Ghosts
of America's
East Coast

Jackie Eileen Behrend

To Abbie,
Happy Hauntings!

Jackie Behrend

CRANE HILL
PUBLISHERS

Cover design by Scott Fuller

Published by Crane Hill Publishers
www.cranehill.com

Printed in Canada

Library of Congress Cataloging-in-Publication Data

Behrend, Jackie Eileen, 1957-
    Ghosts of America's East Coast / by Jackie Eileen Behrend.
       p.cm.
    ISBN 1-57587-168-8 (trade paper)
       1. Ghosts—Atlantic Coast (U.S.) 2. Haunted places—Atlantic
Coast (U.S.) I. Title.

BF1472.U6 B44 2001
133.1'0974—dc21

                                        2001028613

10   9   8   7   6   5   4   3   2   1

For my mother and business partner,
Marlene, with whom I've
photographed the lonely, darkened
regions of the East Coast;
and for my three adorable kitties,
Eli, Beej, and Teader,
who make me laugh every day.

Contents

Introduction

During my research for the book *The Hauntings of Williamsburg, Yorktown, and Jamestown,* I was astonished at the large number of hauntings reported in this historic triangle of Virginia. My extensive studies on ghosts of the region led me to believe that literally hundreds of restless spirits roam the birthplace of our nation.

I learned that ghosts are frequently witnessed throughout the country as well. I was surprised to find just how many spirits walk this great land of ours. These ghostly experiences make for some extraordinary tales.

People of the seventeenth, eighteenth, and nineteenth centuries were convinced that ghosts lived among them. Their sincere beliefs led them to write and speak of ghosts freely, relaying ghost stories at dinner parties and other social gatherings. Only in the twentieth century did people begin hesitating to admit they believed in the supernatural.

Many of the tales I've come across are from the diaries and journals of people who lived long ago. Oddly enough, some of the spirits recorded by previous generations are still being described by people living today. Their reluctance to leave the earth has continued for hundreds of years.

As a ghost tour owner and former tour guide, I found that at least one family always stays after the tour to tell of their own experiences. At book signings I have spent a great deal of time listening to eyewitness accounts of ghostly events. People seem compelled to tell me of their haunted houses or specter-filled work places. This suggests that more and more people are returning to the beliefs of those who came before them. Many have now come to terms with the fact that ghosts truly exist. An avid "ghost hunter," I, too, have had numerous encounters with lingering spirits. In this book, I share many of these experiences, as well as several haunting events told to me by people living along the Eastern Seaboard.

There is no better evidence for proving that spirits remain with us than photographs. The photographs in the following pages were taken by my mother and partner, Marlene, and me in some of the most haunted places in the country. These photos have not been altered in any way.

Many stories in this book give proof to the theory that if you enjoy a person's company in life, you may also enjoy their ghostly presence after death. Unfortunately, the reverse is also possible. Ghosts can have any one of a thousand personalities. Just as a person has little control over whom he works beside, we also have little control over the spirits around us. Friendly or troublesome—it's the luck of the draw.

While contemplating the subject of ghosts, it's important to remember that an entity can still think, even though his body no longer exists. His mind continues to function in another dimension. He may be confused by his surroundings but he continues to have the ability to reason.

For every ghost on earth, there is a separate and distinct reason why he remains. It is impossible to determine all the reasons for hauntings. If you're ever confronted by an unearthly specter, ask yourself why he exists. Perhaps by understanding his reasons for lingering with the living, you will not be frightened by his presence.

The Suffering Spirits of Lake George

L ake George, New York, has been a popular tourist destination since the first resort hotel was built on its shores in 1800. Today, dozens of fine hotels overlook its sparkling waters. Visitors tour the thirty-two-mile lake on one of several charming, old-fashioned boats while enjoying live music and delicious cuisine.

Gazing on the bustling streets of Lake George Village, it's difficult to imagine it the scene of mass death. In August 1757, during the French and Indian War, one of our country's most shameful incidents took place at Fort William Henry, overlooking Lake George.

At the time of the war, much of America was still a harsh wilderness. This made traveling by boat the most favorable, expedient means. Whoever controlled the waters could control the outcome of the war, so French and British forces battled for control of the waterways leading to Canada. The skirmishes on and around the lake are known as The Battle of Lake George.

For the duration of the war, local Indians aided both the British and French in their quests for domination. The armies paid the Indians for the scalps of their enemies. For the most part, the Indians remained loyal to the French.

In the summer of 1757, the battles surrounding Lake George escalated to a fevered pitch. The French enlisted the aid of thirty-three native tribes to attack British colonialists at Fort William Henry. On August 2, eight thousand French and eighteen hundred Indians circled the fort. The terrified inhabitants listened to the sound of native drums as they prayed for their lives and the lives of their families.

As August 3 dawned, French artillery fire opened on the fort. The courageous Colonel George Monro did his best to counter the attack. Tragically, most of his men were too ill to fend off their assailants. They were clearly outnumbered and outmaneuvered. Three hellish days of constant cannon fire took its toll. Fort William Henry was in a desperate situation.

Word of Monro's plight reached his superior, Major General Daniel Webb, at Fort Edward, sixteen miles away. Monro felt confident that Webb, with his army of sixteen hundred troops, would soon come to his aid. Sadly, he was wrong. Under protest from his men, Webb decided it best not to send reinforcements. The soldiers at Fort Edward were forced to do nothing as they listened to the deadly artillery fire in the distance.

Unaware of his commander's decision, Monro continued to wait for assistance. His hopes were dashed when a bloodstained letter was found on a dead scout. The letter stated that Webb had no intention of offering help.

As the assault intensified, Fort William Henry was consumed by fire. Monro knew there was nothing more he could do. He decided his only course of action was to accept the French terms of surrender.

On August 9, 1757, all those able to walk left Fort William Henry under French guard. They were to be held prisoner at Fort Edward, which was by then controlled by the French. French leaders assured their captives that they would be treated fairly and that safe passage to Fort Edward was guaranteed. Those too ill or too injured to travel were to remain in the safety of the fort.

Unbeknownst to the French, upon their departure, their Indian allies stormed Fort William Henry. Without mercy, they scalped the remaining men, women, and children. After the carnage ended, the attackers went to the nearby cemetery and ravaged the graves, scalping and mutilating the dead bodies.

The dead had their revenge. The grave robbers contracted smallpox from the corpses and died lingering deaths.

As hundreds of Indians massacred the inhabitants of Fort William Henry, others crept through the dense forest, preparing to pounce upon the unsuspecting English captives walking to Fort Edward.

Suddenly, thousands of them leapt from the woods, and a savage killing spree ensued. They scalped, stabbed, and tortured the British troops. French soldiers fought to no avail to protect their captives. What is now Lake George Village was a wilderness drenched in blood. It was later found that the tribes committed these atrocities because the French had not paid them for the scalps of their enemies.

In 1760, the war was finally over. The burned-out Fort William Henry was never rebuilt. The forest eventually grew over the site where thousands had perished. Time passed, and no thought was given to the eighteenth-century fort.

Then, two hundred years after the fort's fiery demise, local businessmen built a replica of Fort William Henry on its original site. During the project, archaeologists excavated the fort's cemetery and were shocked by what they found.

Many bodies lying in the graveyard had been hideously butchered. Skulls showed signs of scalping, bodies had been riddled with musket balls and canister shot, and many died from multiple agonizing wounds. Bullets with deep teeth marks were unearthed, giving testament to the intense suffering of the victims.

The tumultuous 1750s also left their mark in a less than physical manner. Mysterious occurrences abound in the vicinity of the mass killings. On certain nights in August, the faint sound of cannon fire can be heard. Screams of terror sometimes fill the air. At times it seems as if the Battle of Lake George took place only yesterday. Literally hundreds of ghosts are known to roam the grounds. Many homeowners in the area have been made frighteningly aware of their presence.

Lillian Patrillo owns a summer home on the rolling hills surrounding Lake George. "We bought our home on the lake in 1964. When my husband, Howard, passed away in 1983, I decided to come back for the summer by myself. I felt perfectly safe here until something happened to change my mind," Lillian says.

"One evening, when I was in bed, I heard a child crying. She sounded so pitiful. It seemed like she was right in the next room. Even though I was a little nervous, I forced myself to get up and go look for her. I thought she'd wandered away from home, as children sometimes do. I searched the house and couldn't find her, so I went back to bed. About an hour later, I saw a ball of light float into my room and stop at the foot of my bed. I was too frightened to move! Then smoke began pouring out of it. The smoke took the shape of a little girl. She was wearing a long, torn dress and she looked so tired and dirty.

"When she began to cry, I guess my motherly instincts took over. I knew I had to comfort her. As I climbed out of bed, she turned back into a ball and floated out of my room and down the stairs. I followed it until it passed through the front door.

"When I got over the shock, I felt such sadness. That little girl was probably looking for her mother. Obviously, she'll never find her. I hope someday someone will help that poor child."

Guests residing in the area hotels and motels have also experienced hauntings. Robin Spears tells of her ghostly encounter while spending the night in a Lake George Village motel. "My husband, John, and I came here on our honeymoon last year," Robin says. "One night I sent John out for some ice. A minute later, I heard heavy footsteps coming toward our room. Then I heard somebody bang on the door. He just about beat the door down. I knew that it wasn't John, because he had a key.

"After the pounding stopped, I saw the doorknob turn. Somebody was trying to break into our room! I ran to the window and peeked through the curtain, but there was nobody there. John got back a few seconds later. When he saw that I was on the verge of hysterics, he tried to comfort me. He explained that anyone at our door would've had to pass him. There was no other way to the stairwell. I wanted to leave, but John said he'd protect us. I said, 'Protect us from what? Ghosts?'"

Another tale comes from a local tavern. "I was unpacking boxes in the cellar when I looked up and saw smoke coming from the keyhole in the door," explains Mark Atlas. "The smoke filled the room, making it almost impossible for me to breathe. It was so thick that I couldn't see my hand in front of my face. The smell of sulfur was so strong that it burned my eyes. I ran for the door and into the hallway. I looked back and saw the room was totally blackened by smoke.

"I ran upstairs to get the manager. I swear I wasn't gone more than a minute. When we got to the cellar, it was completely clear. There was no smoke or smell at all. My boss laughed and said, 'This happens every now and then. You'll get used to it.' I told him, 'Don't hold your breath.'"

Lillian, Robin, and Mark experienced different types of hauntings, but they all agree that the events of the French and Indian War seem to transcend time in the form of these spirits.

In the late 1750s Lake George, New York, was stained by the blood of many a soldier in the French and Indian War. This ghost, captured on film near Fort William Henry, is one of hundreds of soldiers still roaming the area.

Moments of Terror in Hudson Falls

Moving into a new home can be one of life's happiest times. That is, unless your new home is inhabited by an unwelcome spirit.

Surprisingly, many stories of haunted houses end happily. More often than not, the person telling the story actually enjoys the company of his ghostly resident. Some people have even reported that their invisible roommates saved them from some impending disaster. One woman believed her ghost woke her when her house caught fire. She gives credit for the saving of both her life and her home to her caring apparition.

On the other hand, many people say angry spirits actually drove them from their homes. Unfortunately, I had such an experience. The ghost in my first house terrified me.

I grew up in a little city in upstate New York called Glens Falls. It was mild and beautiful in the summer and bitter cold and snowy in the winter. Many of my relatives lived in an even smaller town, Hudson Falls, five miles away.

Each year, our large family got together to watch the Hudson Falls Easter parade. My beloved grandmother Hazel watched the festivities from her second-story window. She was too ill to join us on the street, but we were able to share her company from below.

Good memories of my youth drew me back to live in the tiny township. Unfortunately, with the death of several family members, including my grandmother, Hudson Falls no longer seemed the same. In spite of this, my fiancé, Don, and I continued to fix up our home on LaBarge Street, which had been named after my mother's family almost a century earlier.

When we first moved in, the old house needed a great deal of work. Day in, day out I labored—painting, cleaning, and fixing it up—while Don was at work. I began to sense a mysterious presence in the house, making me feel as if I weren't alone. Unbeknownst to us, the former tenant had died in the bedroom after a lingering illness. The lonely old gentleman had spent several hours each day playing sad melodies on the piano.

As time passed, we became aware that the temperature in the bedroom was well below that in the rest of the house. Don bought an electric heater, but nothing could warm the chilly room.

My cat, B.C., who had been with me since childhood, seemed terrified of the bedroom and refused to enter it. He had always slept with me, but now he just sat at the doorway, staring at the corner of the room.

As the weeks dragged on, I became overwhelmed by sadness while in the bedroom. Sometimes I couldn't force myself out of bed. However, the moment I left the house, I felt fine and was my old cheery self once again.

It was not long before B.C. did nothing but hide under the couch, refusing to eat. He was a robust cat, weighing more than twenty pounds, and missing meals was unusual for him. He looked as if he felt ill, which deeply concerned me. Then other strange happenings followed.

During the day, the lights flickered on and off, as did the appliances. At night we were often awakened by the sound of the television and the glare of the overhead light, both of which we had turned off before going to bed. We grew tired and discouraged.

One evening we asked my Uncle Gene to look in on B.C., because we were going to be out of the house for several hours. Moments after Gene entered the house, he noticed a foul odor. Sensing something was very wrong, Gene decided to leave with B.C. He hastily grabbed the cat and headed for the door. With this, the lights began switching on and off rapidly, which scared Gene out of his wits. Finally, the lights went out completely, leaving Gene in total darkness. He groped for the exit, eventually making his way to the door. He pulled desperately at the knob, but the door wouldn't open. The locks in this old house had to be turned manually, which Gene insisted he had not done.

Panicked, Gene frantically tried to find his way out. After several long minutes, he escaped. My uncle refused to come inside the house ever again, not even to help us move.

Don and I ended up selling most everything we owned just to free ourselves of this cursed home. We moved into a lovely cottage on the banks of the Hudson River and began to live a normal life once more. We found the happiness we had lost, and B.C. got his appetite back.

It has been more than fifteen years since I lived on LaBarge Street, but I will never forget the fright it wreaked. I consider myself lucky to have survived the ordeal with nothing more than an empty wallet and bad memories.

My experience in Hudson Falls is the exception rather than the rule. Most ghosts in residence aren't menacing. Some are so inconspicuous, their presence may go unnoticed. The occasional missing keys may be all you experience from your uninvited entity. Most ghosts are happy amongst the living and don't feel the need to show themselves in any way.

Pets may be the first to know if a spirit dwells inside a home. Cats and dogs seem to sense and even see the spirits around them. How they act toward an entity can reveal the ghost's intentions. If your pet becomes frightened when it walks into a specter-filled room, it may be that the ghost objects to your family's invasion of its territory. If the animal rubs on furniture or wags its tail, then your ghost is probably friendly. Odd behavior in animals is one of the best ways to tell whether you have a spirit among you.

Another indication is sudden temperature changes in your home. If one room is much colder than the rest, this may be where your ghost resides. If you feel considerably less happy than usual while in a particular room, this room may have an unearthly presence. If your mood changes dramatically when you walk into your home, there is a good chance your house contains more than one entity.

If you hear footsteps or other odd noises while alone in the house, don't dismiss it as your imagination. You may have a ghostly resident. A spirit may not be visible, but he can be heard walking or moving about.

Perhaps a door is found open when you know you've closed it, or the faucets turn on by themselves. Don't be frightened—it could just be a ghost carrying on with his daily routine. More often than not, spirits just want to be left alone. When this is the case, it is indeed possible to share your home with them without it disrupting your life.

Pay attention to your feelings. If you feel like you are not alone when no one else is in the house, perhaps you have a ghost. If you get chills on a warm summer evening, you may be in the presence of a spirit.

There are reported cases in which ghosts have actually touched people. The part of the body that was touched felt either a very cold or very hot burning sensation. Physical contact with spirits is uncommon, however.

On rare occasions, people have actually taken on the personality of the ghost occupying their home. If that person has a weak or passive personality, and the ghost has an aggressive and strong nature, there might be a slight chance that this could happen. If you feel you have a ghost in your home, keep your guard up until you can assess his personality. You will be able to tell quickly if it is a menacing spirit.

I would like to be able to say that a ghost cannot hurt you; however, no one can say this with real certainty. With all the ghostly encounters I have experienced (and they have been numerous), I have never been physically harmed. I have been scared half to death by a few apparitions, but so far none of them has inflicted any bodily damage upon me.

Be aware of what goes on around you, but don't automatically think a ghost is the culprit when something is misplaced or missing. Nevertheless, if odd things continue to happen, you may indeed be in the presence of spirits.

A Mother's Love Knows No Bounds

L ove is a powerful motive for a ghost to remain on earth. Some people love a particular person so much, they simply refuse to leave them after death. They prefer to watch over their beloved until it is time for them to meet again in the afterlife.

Bradley Newman from Portland, Maine, related the story of his mother's never-ending love. Bradley's mother died two years ago but apparently has not left her son's side.

Bradley and his wife, Bernice, have noticed several unusual occurrences in the past two years but until recently have ignored them. It was not uncommon for them to be awakened during the night by strange noises. In the mornings, they found household items mysteriously moved from one place to another. Despite these happenings, the Newmans were unwilling to believe that Bradley's mother remained with them in some ghostly form of existence—that is, until one unforgettable night.

That day, Bradley had gone grocery shopping and returned home with his arms full of heavy bags. He set a frozen chicken on the floor by the refrigerator, put the rest of the groceries away, and then proceeded with his daily routine.

About an hour after the couple went to bed that night, they heard a banging sound from the kitchen. The noise was much louder than any of the other peculiar sounds. The couple was so frightened by this that they chose not to investigate the source of the noise. Bradley reasoned that a burglar would have simply left after ransacking their home. He couldn't imagine why the thief was making so much noise and taking so long to complete his task. It wasn't until the next morning that he got his answer.

As the couple cautiously made their way into the kitchen, they found nothing disturbed. Then Bradley noticed the chicken he had purchased the day before had not been put into the freezer. It had remained on the floor by the refrigerator throughout the night. In his haste to put away the groceries, he completely forgot about the bird. He recalled his mother's comments on how unsafe poultry could be if not kept frozen. On more than one occasion, Bradley heard his mother's warning on the dangers of an unfrozen chicken.

Suddenly it all made sense. The ghost of Bradley's mother, as yet another warning, about life's little dangers had made the ruckus the previous night. Bradley now has no doubt that his mother remains in his home, watching over his family. He knows she loved him so much in life that she cannot bear to leave his side, even in death. To this day protecting him—even from beyond the grave.

Skipper, the Ghost Dog of Concord

Concord, New Hampshire, is thought to be the home of numerous eighteenth-century ghosts. This area's rich colonial history has left a haunting mark on the land. However, the grounds of Concord hold more than human spirits. Animal apparitions roam its outskirts as well.

Roger Kline is a native of Concord. He and his wife, Roxanne, find it a wonderful place to raise their six dogs. Their farm outside town gives their frisky pets ample room to run. The couple loves all of their dogs equally, except one. Skipper is the oldest and holds a special place in the Klines' hearts.

Skipper had belonged to Roger's late father, Paul. The little dog was a loyal friend to the elderly man. Paul had been confined to a wheelchair after breaking his hip several years before his death. Skipper spent every day by Paul's side. Roger later found the faithful dog half-starved beside Paul's dead body. Skipper had refused to leave his master's side even though Paul had died from a heart attack days earlier.

Roger took Skipper home. However, it took quite a while for the mournful beagle to fit in with the rest of the family. He just couldn't seem to get over the death of his best friend. It seemed that no matter what the Klines did to cheer him up, Skipper continued to suffer from a broken heart. Finally, after several weeks, Skipper began to show signs of life. Within a year, the little beagle was back to his old perky self, thanks to the kindness of his new owners.

Skipper's life was perfect except for one thing: He had been kept inside most of the time, since Paul seldom left his home. Life with the Klines was a different story. The couple worked all day and put their dogs out until they returned home in the evening. It was obvious that Skipper didn't approve of this arrangement. Roger practically had to drag Skipper out of the house each morning.

To make the transition from the inside to the outside easier for Skipper, Roger built an elaborate doghouse for him. He filled it with squeak toys and the blanket Paul had given the beagle years earlier. Skipper adapted eventually. In time, he even welcomed the time he spent outdoors.

When the Klines returned home in the evening, it was plain to see that Skipper had spent a fun-filled day. His food bowl was turned over, the squeak toys were spread all over the lawn, and his blanket looked as if it had been in a tug of war. Several years passed, and all was well in Skipper Kline's life.

Then one evening, when the Klines arrived home from work, they found Skipper asleep on his blanket. That was unusual, because he always greeted his people with a hardy welcome. When Roger tried to wake his little dog, he found that Skipper had died some-time during the day.

Although the Klines knew Skipper had lived a long, healthy life, they were filled with sorrow by his passing. They loved their sweet animal so much that the loss they felt was tremendous. The couple knew their favorite four-legged companion would never again be waiting to greet them. They buried Skipper's body beside his dog-house and placed his blanket and toys inside.

The next evening when they returned home, they were shocked by what they found. Skipper's toys were spread all over the lawn, and his blanket was in a mangled heap. Since the other family dogs were kept elsewhere, the couple couldn't imagine what had hap-pened to Skipper's things. Bewildered, they tidied up the doghouse and walked the fifty yards to their front door.

As the couple reached the doorway, they heard a familiar bark. It was Skipper! The Klines turned and ran back to the empty dog-house. They could hardly believe their eyes. Skipper's toys were tossed about and his blanket was lying in a rumpled heap.

From that day forward, the Klines have placed Skipper's things neatly inside his doghouse before leaving for work each morning.

Most often upon their return, they find the things spread all over the lawn. The couple now believes that the bond between humans and their beloved pets cannot be broken, even in death.

Revolutionary Warship Sails off Salem's Shores

Salem, Massachusetts, is best known for its witch trials of 1692. The insanity began when several local girls accused various townspeople of putting spells on them. By October of that year, more than one hundred people had come under suspicion of practicing witchcraft.

If a person confessed to the crime of witchery, as fifty of the accused did, they were spared the painful death of hanging. Of those who would not confess, nineteen were hanged and one was pressed to death with boulders.

The witch trials ended abruptly when the governor's wife became one of those accused. Although the witch hunting madness was over, several unfortunate citizens lingered in jail for months before being acquitted. As a final indignity, the prisoners were forced to pay for the time they had spent behind bars. They were even made to pay for the chains that bound them. It was indeed a sad and shameful time in Salem's history.

Except for the time of the witch hunts, Salem has been much like any other seaside New England town. Fishing and shipping have played a large part in its economy. Along with fishermen and merchants, pirates and privateers were known to sail throughout Salem's waterways. They terrorized those aboard sailing vessels off the Massachusetts coast.

Privateering was licensed during the time of the Revolution to encourage the robbing and sinking of British warships. Many an English sailor met with a deadly fate in the waters near Salem. Not surprisingly, ghostly remnants of this time in history are known to linger off Salem's shores.

Throughout the years, a large eighteenth-century British ship has been seen sailing amongst the numerous recreational boats in Salem's waterways. Its ominous presence has frightened dozens, if not hundreds of boaters. The ship comes dangerously close to the other boats.

One Salem resident and frequent boater, Martin Saigebrook, claims to have come face to face with the Revolutionary warship. His terrifying ordeal took place on a hot July night in 1997. Martin explains, "My wife and I were having such a good time that we decided to stay afloat well after dark. Everyone else had already gone home. The water was calm and the moon was bright, so we didn't think there was any danger.

"All of a sudden, a heavy fog rolled in. Then a huge wave almost capsized us. A minute later, we saw a massive ship about twenty-five feet away. It didn't look like any ship I'd ever seen before. It was wooden with a tall mast. You may not believe this, but I swear it had cannons pointed straight at us. To tell you the truth, we were too scared to try to get out of the line of fire. We just stood there wondering what was going to happen next.

"A little while later, I'm not exactly sure how long, the fog cleared and the ship disappeared right before our eyes. We hurried to shore and we've never sailed after dark since."

Perhaps the Revolutionary warship seeks revenge for its merciless destruction. It may be that its dead seamen are looking for the privateers who doomed them to a watery grave. Whatever the reason, it seems the waters hold more than the boats of modern times. If you plan to sail off Salem's coastline, it might be to your advantage to dock before sunset. If not, who knows what deadly forces you may encounter.

The Guarded Graveyard
of Boston

Ghosts inhabit literally hundreds of places. One of the most obvious is a graveyard. Throughout the centuries, graveyards have been known to hold long-forgotten spirits, ghosts that have followed their bodies to their final resting place. There are numerous theories as to why this might be.

One explanation is that a person was so attached to the physical side of life that he cannot bear to leave his body behind. Perhaps he does not believe in an afterlife, so he remains with the only life force he knows and recognizes—his body.

Another thought is that perhaps a soul wishes to remain with the family he loved and was buried near. Perhaps he loved one or more of these people so much, that he literally cannot bring himself to leave their side. He may not believe there is a chance of meeting them in some other form of existence. To him, the bodies of his family are all he has left.

Graveyard hauntings also may be territorial. A ghost who roams the grounds where his body lies may feel a sense of security that comes from the land. Perhaps he feels the body was the vessel of life; therefore, where his body remains is home. It is for this reason that the angry spirit of the Saunders family graveyard is thought to linger. The small cemetery sits near the western edge of Boston.

Raymond Saunders, his wife, their seven children, and his elderly mother moved from Salem to Boston during the mid-nineteenth century. Raymond was extremely protective of the family's privacy. No family member was ever allowed visitors. They all seemed to live a very sad and lonely existence. Remarkably, Raymond outlived his wife, mother, and all but two of his children.

Since his demise Raymond Saunders' ghost continues to protect the privacy of his deceased family. Passersby have heard his authoritative voice as they walked the grounds of his former home. He has even been known to toss small stones and twigs at people who dare wander onto the property.

Thelma Reeves from Springfield, Massachusetts, was visiting her daughter, Mary, on a sunny day in October of 2000. They were strolling through the streets of Boston, admiring the fall foliage. As they passed a small graveyard obscurely tucked beside a grove of trees, their curiosity was piqued. They had walked this street on many occasions but never had noticed the tiny cemetery. Thelma and Mary decided to take a closer look. Thelma recalls the events of that day.

"As we approached the graveyard, I could see the name 'Saunders' engraved on a tall headstone," Thelma explains. "Suddenly a cold breeze began to blow. It was unusually strong. When we got to the gate and looked inside, we began to hear a strange noise. It sounded like a man shouting. Even though his voice was faint, I could tell he was angry. We looked all over, but no one was anywhere around. Mary said we should go, so we turned to walk away. Just then, I felt something hit me in the back. I looked down and saw a small rock lying on the ground by my feet. Then, a second later, I saw another rock fly past my head. This one was much bigger than the one I saw on the ground. It missed me by inches. Ever since then, when Mary and I pass by the Saunders' graveyard, we just keep on walking."

Perhaps the ghost of Raymond Saunders feels the land in which his family is interred is his territory. He may feel threatened by the presence of visitors.

If you spot the Saunders family graveyard while strolling the streets of Boston, it might be wise to do as Thelma Reeves does and keep on walking. And if you simply can't resist exploring, watch out for flying stones!

This angry ghost dwells in the Saunders family graveyard in Boston. Could it be the spirit of Raymond Saunders, the protective father who denied his wife and children any visitors even in life?

Angels Come
in Many Forms

On one of our many sightseeing trips together in the north-eastern countryside, my mother and I found ourselves in a terrible predicament. As we drove through Connecticut's rolling hills, we managed to get hopelessly lost.

Floundering from road to road, we were running low on gas. Suddenly, steam began to spew from the engine, soon leaving our car immobile. The radiator had sprung a leak, stranding us on the side of the road. It was 1:30 a.m., and no help was in sight.

A teenager at the time, I had the awful feeling that we would remain lost for days. The landscape was devoid of houses or businesses, and we had no idea which direction to turn.

About two hours into our ordeal, we noticed a rickety old truck approaching. I thought to myself that I could walk faster than it was moving. After it stopped beside us, two elderly gentlemen dressed in dirty overalls emerged from the truck.

The men seemed to know instinctively of our problem, as one of them was carrying a can of radiator sealant. The other held a jug of water in his hand. They quickly fixed our car so we could get on our way. We told them of our fuel shortage, and they kindly guided us to a gas station. By this time we were incredibly tired, so they directed us to a nearby hotel.

The next morning we felt rested and refreshed, thrilled that we were headed home. Mom and I began to talk about the night before and its amazing coincidences. It seemed as if good fortune had smiled on us in our time of need.

On our way out of the area, we approached the same gas station where we had gotten fuel hours earlier. Mom stood on the brakes and said in disbelief, "This station looks like it's been closed for years!" The windows were boarded up, and the pumps were covered with mud.

We got out of the car and walked around the building. It was then that we came across the old truck that had carried our helpers the night before. As we got closer, we could see that its wheels were missing. The windshield was shattered, and the interior was torn. It was easy to see that this truck was useless. We were so shocked that we could hardly believe our eyes. For a short while, we even wondered whether we had imagined the whole thing.

As we gazed upon the broken-down station, we knew some unknown force had helped us. Could our guardian angels have taken the form of two kindly old men who rescued us from the perils of the night? Whenever I feel lost, I think back to that extraordinary night and find comfort in the fact that we are never really alone.

A Colonial Party Continues at Newport

Newport, Rhode Island, an upscale summer resort, has been host to some of America's most prominent families. It is thought to be the yachting capital of the Eastern Seaboard. In the summer, Newport is a place where people party and let down their hair.

The area first became a popular destination for tourists in the early 1700s, when South Carolinians discovered it to be a pleasant place to escape the summer heat. From that time forward, Newport has been inundated with fun-loving visitors.

Seaworthy vessels easily accessed Newport, rendering it vulnerable to enemy forces. During the Revolution, British troops occupied the city from 1776 to 1779. They promptly moved into its colonial homes, often leaving them virtually destroyed. They vandalized the city and terrorized its citizens.

The three years of enemy occupation pushed Newport to the edge of destruction. Fortunately, in 1780, Comte de Rochambeau, with a force of four thousand French soldiers, helped evict the unwelcome British. Although Newport needed much restoration, its citizens were finally free to rebuild their lives.

During the occupation, drunken enemy troops gathered in the streets, harassed the women as they passed, and burned furniture as firewood in the center of town.

Dozens of rowdy soldiers crowded around the smoldering fires while drinking stolen liquor from local taverns. At times, the parties grew out of control. Troops fought amongst themselves and threatened all those daring to come near.

Since the eighteenth century, Newport has carried remnants of its tumultuous past. On balmy summer nights, the air is sometimes filled with the sound of a raucous party. The glow of a fire can be seen in certain sections of town. Strangely, the rowdy get-togethers aren't found in local bars, and the mysterious glow of unseen fires doesn't come from celebratory fireworks. Townspeople can't seem to find a rational explanation for these extraordinary events.

Many of Newport's citizens, including Tamara Barns, believe the source of the festivities is of a supernatural nature. Tamara recalls, "One night last summer, while I was walking home from work, I heard loud voices and laughter. There was a strange glow lighting up the sky in front of me. I didn't want to turn the corner and walk down the street where all this was going on, but I had to get home. There was no way to avoid it, so I prepared myself for the worst.

"You can imagine my surprise when I found the street totally empty. It was dark and really quiet. There was nobody around but me. Even though everything turned out fine that night, I've found a new route to walk home from work. A girl can't be too careful nowadays."

Those looking for a quiet, uneventful vacation in Newport had better beware of strange activity on balmy summer nights. And if it's a party they're looking for, they might just find one.

During British occupation, Newport found itself at the mercy of unruly soldiers. Fueled by stolen liquor, they gathered in the streets and terrorized the town. More than two centuries later, these spirits obviously don't know the party is over.

The Death Bed

Inanimate objects can indeed hold spirits of the past. Ghosts can actually follow pieces of furniture as they are moved from house to house. Linda Brea of Cape May, New Jersey, reached an agreement with the spirits making a home in her bed.

"For centuries, my family members took to this bed when their time to die had come," Linda explains. "Several people in my family have spent their last days in what we call 'the death bed.'

"It had been several years since one of my relatives passed away in the bed, so I thought it had outlived its purpose. Since I needed a bed in my new apartment, I moved the deathbed from our old family farmhouse to my new place. The very first night the bed was in my apartment, strange things began to happen.

"That night, when I started to undress, I sat on the edge of the bed to remove my shoes. Suddenly, I felt the mattress sink down like someone was lying next to me. I saw the imprint of a human body outlined on the bed! I ran out of the room and spent the rest of the night on the couch. The next morning I felt ridiculous. I decided the weird things that happened the night before had to have been in my imagination. After all, I've heard so many strange stories about the bed that it's only natural for me to be a little suspicious.

"I finally screwed up my courage and went back into the bedroom. I couldn't believe what I saw! The room was a total disaster. The clothes from my closet were all over the floor, and the rest of my stuff was scattered everywhere.

"Ever since then, I've learned to deal with my haunted bed," Linda said laughingly. "Before I go to sleep each night, I warn the ghosts around me that I will burn the bed if they give me any more trouble. Now the only strange thing that happens is that the covers are pulled off of me every now and then."

To Linda's relief, the spirits have settled into a routine. They now feel right at home, just as they did in the old family farmhouse.

Franklin Court Holds a Colonial Mystery

Philadelphia is probably best known as the birthplace of democracy. Its colonial buildings are well preserved for all to see. The people of Philadelphia are proud of their heritage and the large part their city played in shaping our great nation.

During the eighteenth century, everyone who was anyone spent time in Philadelphia. Thomas Jefferson, George Washington, and Patrick Henry were familiar names and faces among those of Pennsylvania's most progressive township. But of all the influential people in colonial Philadelphia, probably the best loved and admired was Benjamin Franklin.

In his lifetime, Franklin purchased very little real estate. In 1763, on what is now Franklin Court, in Philadelphia, construction began on the only home he ever owned. A steel frame marks the spot where his three-story house once stood. Glass tubes have been placed inside the frame to allow visitors to view the original foundations. Unfortunately, nothing more remains of the building where Franklin spent his last days—nothing physical anyway.

Benjamin Franklin believed that "early to bed, early to rise makes a man healthy, wealthy, and wise." He adhered to this philosophy and lived his life accordingly. He was known to rise well before dawn and walk the streets of his neighborhood.

People who lived in the area spoke of hearing Franklin's heavy footsteps on the cobblestones in the early morning hours. He was also known to whistle while he walked the darkened streets of Philadelphia. These sometimes annoying habits are thought not to have ended with Franklin's death.

Just before sunrise over Franklin Court, footsteps are often heard from the reconstructed courtyard. The whistling of a happy tune can also be detected in nearby buildings. People have even reported catching a glimpse of the great man himself as he passes throughout the streets.

A local policeman, who doesn't wish to be identified for professional reasons, says he witnessed Franklin's ghost one morning just before dawn. "I was patrolling the area near Franklin Court when I saw someone dressed in colonial clothing," the policeman explains. "I didn't think much of it, because it's not unusual to see colonial costumes here in Philadelphia.

"He was whistling too loud for that hour of the morning, so I got out of the car to catch up with him on foot. I needed to tell him to keep it down. He was walking slowly and with a cane, so I knew it wouldn't take me long to reach him. I called out to him, but he ignored me. He finally turned a corner and out of sight.

"It was only a couple of seconds before I turned the same corner. He should've been right in front of me, but he wasn't. If he weren't a ghost, there'd be no explanation for his disappearance other than he sprouted wings and flew away."

Was this the ghost of Benjamin Franklin or just a clever imposter? Perhaps if you walk Franklin Court just before dawn, you may learn the answer to this question for yourself.

The "Spirited" Horse
of Brandywine Valley

Brandywine Valley in southeastern Pennsylvania was a haven for early settlers. They flocked to the banks of the Brandywine River because of its fertile ground. Its rolling hills were a perfect place to grow their crops and raise their children.

In the autumn of 1777, this picturesque valley became the scene of a battle. During the Revolutionary War, General George Washington and his troops met General William Howe's British forces on the grounds of Brandywine Valley. A bloody fight ensued. The brutal tug of war ended in victory for the British.

The remnants of those tremulous days in September can be found on the deadly field of battle. They are not seen in the form of ghostly soldiers or in the faint echoes of cannon fire. They aren't found in the homes that sheltered Washington and the Marquis de Lafayette. Oddly enough, they are witnessed in the misty form of a lone horse.

The ravages of war affect all living creatures—not just humans. The horse, perhaps, suffers the most of all animals in war. Since the horse is a multifunctional animal, it has been dragged into battle for centuries. Forced to charge the enemy, it more often has felt the sting of a bullet than its rider has. The fighting in Brandywine Valley was no exception. Many frightened horses were sacrificed for the cause of freedom. It is believed to be one of these magnificent beasts that haunts the area to this very day.

Witnesses say they've seen the ghost of a smoky gray stallion galloping throughout the rolling hills of Delaware County. Cindy Rhodes, a longtime resident of the area, has tried to help this panic-stricken apparition. "My friends and I were out riding last fall when we saw a horse in trouble," Cindy explains. "He had no rider and

didn't seem to know where he was going. He was just running aimlessly. I thought he'd probably jumped a fence and gotten lost.

"I knew if we cornered him, I could rope him and take him back
to the stables. We rode after him and managed to back him up
against some trees. I know the area like the back of my hand, so I
knew exactly where to drive him. There was no way he could've gotten away from us. I don't know how it happened, but we lost him. If
you ask me, it was impossible for him to shake us. We were right on
his tail, and somehow he vanished without a trace. We searched for a
long time, but came up with nothing. That animal had to have been
either a magician or a ghost."

The frightened apparition has shown itself in the presence of
dozens of people for over two centuries. Perhaps some day he will
find the path leading him out of the line of fire and into peace.

*Though the Revolutionary War ended more than two hundred years ago, the "spirited" horse
of Brandywine Valley still gallops the fields in noble service.*

Death on the First Day's Battle

During the first three days of July 1863, the largest military campaign waged on North American soil took place in the small town of Gettysburg, Pennsylvania. More than fifty-three thousand casualties resulted from the battle. It was literally the turning point of the Civil War. Until then, the Confederate Army had taken control of most battlefields on which they fought against Union forces.

The massive battle at Gettysburg was an unfortunate accident. The meeting of opposing troops had not been planned. The Federal and Confederate Armies literally collided on the outskirts of town. Confederate General Robert E. Lee and his army of seventy-five thousand men stopped in Gettysburg for supplies—principally shoes. The Union Army, commanded by General George Gordon Meade, numbered about eighty-eight thousand men.

On the first day of fighting, the Confederates took control of the battlefield. They managed to push the Union forces back through town. The second day of battle was a draw; on the third day, the Union Army clearly came out ahead.

It is believed that with such massive death having occurred in Gettysburg, ghostly occurrences abound. Some people feel that the past moves along with the present in another dimension parallel to our own. They contend that the horrific events of the Civil War, as well as its ghosts, live on in Gettysburg.

Perhaps some of these ghosts linger on the battlefields out of a sense of duty. They may be unwilling to leave until they've successfully completed their jobs. This is believed to be the reason for the haunting of McPherson's Ridge on the western edge of town.

The commander of the Union 1st Corps, Major General John Reynolds, never ran from a fight—no matter the odds. His men credited him with undaunted courage and would follow him anywhere. He never asked them to do anything he wouldn't do himself.

On the morning of the first day's battle, as Reynolds rode along McPherson's Ridge, he saw the Confederates advancing through the woods. He knew that a desperate move had to be made or he and his men would soon be overtaken. Reynolds formed the troops in a line and ordered them to charge the woods. Unafraid of the consequences, he led the attack.

The enemy was too strong for the Union . They met Reynolds' soldiers head-on, inflicting numerous casualties. It wasn't long before the Rebels took control of the field. While sitting tall in the saddle, Reynolds unnecessarily exposed himself to the enemy and was struck in the back of the neck by a Minie ball. He died instantly.

From that day forward, it seems General Reynolds' spirit has continued the attack against the Confederate Army. On McPherson's Ridge, off the Chambersburg Pike, a ghostly figure on horseback has been seen on numerous occasions. With his sword held high, he leads the attack. Witnesses say that on still nights they can hear him call out from the darkness. Some swear they've heard, "Forward, men!"

The loss incurred by Reynolds' forces notwithstanding, the Union did have one significant victory over the Confederates that day. Where the Chambersburg Pike formed the railroad cut in a ravine, the Union Army trapped two hundred Confederate soldiers. Most of those helpless men lost their lives in that ravine.

The small Union victory of that day has left its mark in a physical and a ghostly manner. The bones of one Confederate recently were found protruding from the side of the railroad cut.

Perhaps the bones of this Rebel soldier are not all that remains of him. The glowing image of a man walking through the deadly ravine is seen from time to time. Could he possibly be searching for his missing remains? He may not be aware that his broken body has been found and finally laid to rest at the National Cemetery.

The Haunting Experiences of the 20th Maine

Throughout the second day's battle of July 2, 1863, in Gettysburg, hundreds of northern soldiers spoke of witnessing the ghost of our first President, George Washington. The colonel who wrote of this amazing encounter was none other than Joshua Chamberlain, commander of the 20th Maine and hero of Little Round Top. Chamberlain wrote, "All things, even the most common were magnified and made mysterious by the strange spell of night . . . Now, from a dark angle of the roadside came a whisper, whether from earthly or unearthly voice one cannot feel quite sure, that the form of Washington had been seen that afternoon at sunset riding over the Gettysburg hills."

The Union soldiers who saw Washington's apparition were filled with a renewed sense of encouragement. Their haunting experience made them feel as if they were destined to win the war. They began to believe they could overcome the devastating losses of the first day's battle and emerge victorious.

What the men of the 20th Maine didn't realize at the time was that they were to play a crucial role in turning the tide of the war in favor of the Union. The unshakable leadership of Chamberlain and his famous bayonet charge down the southern slope of Little Round Top on the second day of battle saved the day for the Union Army. Heavily outnumbered and almost out of ammunition, the 20th Maine was in a desperate situation. The brave and relentless men of the 15th Alabama had made one charge after another up the tree-lined slope of Little Round Top. They were determined to eliminate the 20th Maine, or at least move them from their position. The Confederates never gave up, in spite of the fact that the climb was steep and treacherous.

The 20th Maine had been sent to defend the left flank of the Union line on Little Round Top. Unfortunately for them, the 15th Alabama, led by Colonel William Oates, pushed them back from their position five times. The men of the 20th Maine were dying in alarming numbers. The body count rose by the minute.

Colonel Chamberlain had been ordered not to retreat under any circumstances. If he did, the Confederate Army could maneuver themselves behind the Union line and gain control of the battlefield.

A ghostly haze presides over Little Round Top in Gettysburg. Some believe the soldiers of the Union's 20th Maine found the courage to keep fighting after seeing George Washington's spirit on their way to battle.

This would have been a devastating blow for the Union. Chamberlain and his men were to stand their ground "to the last."

It looked hopeless for the 20th Maine. They knew that, because they were out of ammunition, they could not defend their position from one more Confederate charge. They were facing certain death. Only a bold and daring move could save the day. Chamberlain didn't know what to do. After all, he had been in charge of his unit for only three days, giving new meaning to the phrase "on-the-job training."

Suddenly, an outrageous idea struck Chamberlain. He ordered his men to fix bayonets and charge down the hillside like a swinging door. He wanted his men to sweep the 15th Alabama down the slope and away from the left flank of the Union line. His men thought Chamberlain had gone mad. Could such a drastic tactic ever work? The answer to this question was a resounding "Yes." The bedraggled 20th Maine won the battle and captured hundreds of Confederates. No one would have thought it possible.

What was the force behind the fearless men of the 20th Maine? Some believe it was the bold leadership of Colonel Joshua Chamberlain that kept his men going. Others feel the desperate circumstances that drove the Federals to attempt this daring maneuver. Still others think it was the spirit of George Washington that inspired the men to keep fighting.

Some ghosts showed themselves during the rage of battle at Gettysburg. Perhaps they felt such a strong sense of duty that they returned to finish the fight in which they lost their lives. On Little Round Top during the second day's battle, the 20th Maine was again visited by a haunting presence that encouraged them to victory.

At least one soldier who lost his life on the southern slope of Little Round Top may have returned after death to continue the fight. Colonel Joshua Chamberlain again experienced a sighting for which he could find no explanation. Chamberlain wrote, "There was one fine young fellow, who had been cut down early in the fight with a ghastly wound across his forehead . . . So I had sent him back to our little field hospital, at least to die in peace. Within a half-hour, in a desperate rally I saw that noble youth amidst the rolling smoke as an apparition from the dead . . . in the thick of the fight . . . pressing on as they that shall see death no more."

Chamberlain could have been mistaken about the boy dying in the field hospital. Perhaps the youth was not hurt as badly as the colonel had believed. Nevertheless, if the soldier had survived his gaping head wound, he would not have been discharged from the hospital so soon. The doctors likely would not have let him simply get up and walk back into battle.

In addition, the soldier could not have made it to the hospital, had his wound treated, and then returned to Little Round Top in only thirty minutes. And significant blood loss would have prevented him from resuming his duties. Finally, such a head wound would have likely left the youth too dazed to find his way back through the smoke and chaos.

This unexplainable incident has led many people to believe that some of those killed in battle did return to fight. Their loyalty and bravery did not end merely with their tragic demise.

How the Slaughter Pen Got Its Name

Not all the fighting on Little Round Top took place on its southern slope. On the second day at Gettysburg, a fierce battle was fought on the western slope, looking down over the area known as the Slaughter Pen. The battlefield was so named because of the high death toll of Texas and Alabama troops. The Union also met with great losses there.

The Federals, led by General Gouverneur Warren, held the high ground. The Confederates, whose leader was Major General John Hood, were near the base of Little Round Top, in the area known as Devil's Den.

It is thought that the Confederates fought magnificently that day. If you've ever been on Little Round Top, looking over its rocky cliff, you'd know why this is said. Rebel soldiers ran up the incredibly steep and rocky hill and still had the energy to fight. On that hot day, the Confederates had to carry and load heavy muskets while charging up the hill. They also had to dodge bullets and cannon fire from the Union troops above them.

The courage of the Texans and Alabamians was astounding. Those who made it to the top of the hill fought a brutal hand-to-hand fight with the Union soldiers. During the entire three days of battle, some of the most savage fighting occurred on the western slope of Little Round Top.

Both sides paid a horrible price for their bravery that afternoon. Fragments of a shell that exploded above him hit Hood, severely wounding him. Several Federal officers were hit by artillery fire as well. In spite of the fact that their leaders were dying at an alarming rate, Union forces managed to ward off the Confederate attack and hold their position.

The dramatic events of that fateful day seem to live on in an unusually large number of hauntings. From the slope of Little Round Top to the boulders of Devil's Den, dozens of ghostly figures are known to walk the Slaughter Pen daily. Literally hundreds of haunting events have been recounted throughout the years.

On this bloody ground, my mother and I took several ghostly photographs. It seems that if a person were to walk the area at night, taking pictures randomly, he is bound to capture at least one of these lingering entities on film. They are everywhere.

Some people who have walked the darkened grounds of the Slaughter Pen claim to have spoken with spirits, some of which have appeared in human form. These lost souls will never see the end of the fighting.

If you have the nerve, walk through the Slaughter Pen some evening and take pictures. You might end up with some photographs you simply will not believe. Keep in mind that ghost hunting, however, is not for the squeamish. You never know what frightening spectacle you may encounter.

After the fighting ended in the Slaughter Pen, darkness covered the battlefield. The dead lay sprawled on the ground. The glowing moon illuminated their bodies, making them look as if they were only sleeping. All was quiet.

Dozens of wounded Texans and Alabamians crawled to the stream known as Plum Run, which passes through the base of Little Round Top. They drank the cool water and used it to sooth their agonizing wounds. Many died on the banks of the stream. Its clear water soon turned red from the blood of the dead and wounded.

Suddenly, the song "When This Cruel War Is Over" emanated from a nearby battlefield. Although it was a Confederate singing, the song comforted the Union men. They cheered and gave thanks to the anonymous crooner. For one brief moment, Union and Confederate troops seemed to put their differences aside. Every man atop Little Round Top and down in Devil's Den yearned for home and family. Unfortunately, the only way some of the melancholy men would return home was in a coffin.

Since the night of the second day's battle, the Slaughter Pen has held more than the ghosts of that terrible day. At times, in the stillness of the night, a faint rendition of "When This Cruel War Is Over" can be heard drifting over the land. Not one person has been able to explain this strange phenomenon.

Researchers have placed video recorders at Wheatfield, Little Round Top, and the Slaughter Pen; they have hidden behind boulders and trees, attempting to discover the unknown singer. To their frustration, not one of their efforts has succeeded.

The only explanation is that the intense emotion the men felt while listening to the song has been imprinted on the area. The land seems to have soaked up the events of that day, and it replays them over and over again.

A shape eerily similar to a skull floats over the grounds of the Slaughter Pen at Gettysburg.

The Ghost
of Jennie Wade

Amazingly, Jennie Wade was the only civilian killed during the three days of battle at Gettysburg. She was staying at her sister Georgina's home on Baltimore Street, because Georgina had recently given birth. Jennie was helping care for the baby and tend to the daily chores.

On the morning of her death, July 3, 1863, Jennie told her sister that she felt extremely lucky to be in the safety of their home instead of on the battlefield outside. A short while later, Jennie lay crumpled on the kitchen floor with a bullet in her back.

That morning the town was filled with thousands of Confederate and Union soldiers. The fighting took place on the streets near Georgina's home. The citizens of Gettysburg hid in their basements, terrified that the shower of bullets might strike them and their families. They suddenly found their homes under siege, with bullets hitting the walls of every room.

Jennie Wade did not take cover like most of her neighbors. As Jennie stood in the kitchen baking bread, a stray bullet passed through two doors, killing her instantly. The bullet holes in the doors are visible even today. Jennie was just twenty years old.

After the accident, a Union soldier carried the body to the basement, where it lay for two days. Jennie was then buried in the backyard. Two years later, her body was moved to Evergreen Cemetery, where it remains to this day.

Not surprisingly, some who visit what is known as the Jennie Wade House believe Jennie's spirit did not move on with her body, but in fact lingers on the grounds where her young life ended.

Since the mid-1860s, Jennie's ghost, dressed in black, has been witnessed passing through the walls of her sister's former home. She sometimes hovers over the grounds on which she spent her last days and pays visits to the Old Town museum directly behind the house.

Some tourists say they haven't seen her but have sensed her presence. They say they feel as if they are being watched as they pass from room to room.

During a visit to the Jennie Wade House, my mother and I had an unusual experience of our own. Before entering the home, we took several photographs of the outside of the building. At that point, our cameras worked fine; however, when we stopped to take a picture inside the kitchen where Jennie died, our cameras jammed. The flashes didn't work and the film failed to advance. Moments after leaving the building, our cameras worked once again. Coincidence? Maybe Jennie Wade is just shy.

The only civilian killed at Gettysburg, Jennie Wade was struck down by a stray bullet at age twenty. To this day she seeks the safety of her sister's house. Tourists have also sensed her presence and seen her in the Old Town museum behind the house.

The Phantom Troops of Pickett's Charge

On the hot afternoon of July 3, 1863, at Pickett's Charge, about fifteen thousand Confederates marched through the open battlefield with remarkable courage. They walked in a continuous wave for about a mile, all the while being shot at from every direction.

They began their bold march at Seminary Ridge, planning to attack Union forces stationed atop the hill known as Cemetery Ridge. More than seven thousand Union soldiers, manning one hundred eighteen cannons and seventeen hundred muskets, waited on Cemetery Ridge for the enemy to get within two hundred yards so that they could open fire. Suddenly, the muskets fired and the cannons roared. Entire Confederate regiments were wiped out in one brief moment.

Pickett's Charge was such a devastating loss to the Confederate Army that they never recovered. Many historians believe Pickett's Charge literally changed the course of history.

It was on this extraordinary battlefield that my mother and I took several astounding pictures. Not only did we get photographic proof of the stories written in this book, we also experienced several ghostly encounters.

One moonlit night, as we walked through the cold mud, we happened upon a phantom group of Confederate soldiers. These men are thought to have been killed within moments of each other by either a cannonball or musket fire.

Most Confederate regiments were made up of soldiers from the same hometowns. Many served with their brothers, fathers, and sons. Side by side they fought, slept, and ate. It's entirely possible that they chose to remain together throughout eternity.

If you have the nerve, take your cameras and walk the battlefield of Pickett's Charge after dark. You may be lucky, or unlucky, enough to stumble upon the phantom soldiers.

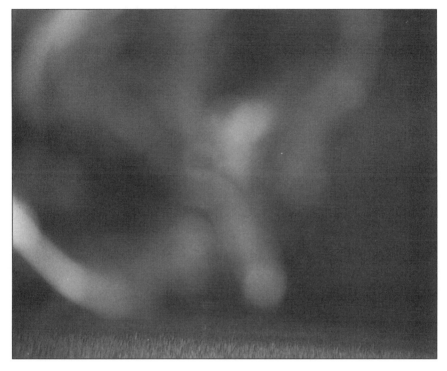

Can you see the face of the smiling soldier of Pickett's Charge?

The phantom troops are not the only spirits you might encounter on the grounds of Pickett's Charge. Others roam the empty field as well.

As we took nighttime photographs of the area, we came upon a curious and mischievous pair of ghosts. Although we weren't able to see them physically, they made their presence known, to us. Walking from the Union line at Cemetery Ridge, I got the strangest feeling that we were being followed. I quickly turned to snap a photograph. Farther into the field, that strange feeling kept getting stronger. After twenty minutes, we decided it was time to leave, so we turned and began walking out of the battlefield.

We had walked farther than we realized. The road seemed a good distance away. On the way back, I quickly turned to take another photograph of the spirits following us. When my camera flashed, I said jokingly, "Gotcha." Apparently, the stalking spirits didn't appreciate this, as thirty seconds later my camera began to flash by itself.

This particular camera requires several steps before you can take a picture. The film has to be manually advanced, and the flash button has to be pushed before you can take a nighttime photograph. The front cover of the camera closes after each picture and has to be manually opened before another one can be taken. As you can imagine, taking a photo with this camera takes quite a bit of effort. It just doesn't go off accidentally.

It was not until the pictures were developed that my mother and I physically saw the ghosts that had followed us for more than a mile that night. Perhaps the spirited soldiers were bored and found us an interesting diversion. Or perhaps they felt threatened by our presence. No one can say for certain. But what I can say for sure is that the ghosts of Pickett's Charge knowingly and deliberately do follow visitors as they walk throughout the battlefield. My photographs are my proof.

Mom and I have taken ghostly photographs throughout the East Coast. We have dozens of startling photos proving that spirits really do exist. Through experience, I've learned that when a spirit is near, I get a heavy feeling on my chest as if something is pushing against my ribs. This is when I take my photographs.

On our first ghost hunt at Pickett's Charge, we became entangled in the plowed-under crops. We made quite a spectacle of ourselves as we tried to leave the field. We hurdled fences and fell into hidden streams. At one point, we got so tickled by our situation that we began to laugh loudly. Instantly, I got that heavy feeling pressing against my chest. I quickly turned and took a photograph of the spirit I felt was behind me.

When this picture was developed, the presence of the smiling soldier was discovered. Apparently, he had come to watch the silly spectacle we were creating. Perhaps this means that even though the ghosts of Pickett's Charge tragically lost their lives, they still haven't lost their sense of humor.

Not all the ghosts found at Pickett's Charge are as friendly as the smiling soldier. On our last ghost hunt there, we were literally confronted by a massive spirit with a less-than-pleasant personality.

As we made our way through the field, I once again felt the pressing against my chest. I knew we were not alone. I took several photographs, thinking one was bound to show the spirit somewhere beside me. Then through my camera lens I saw a menacing ghost approximately three feet away. I had never before witnessed such a sight! He was so enormous that the flash lit him up like a Christmas tree. He stood over six feet tall, and was about three feet wide. The frightening thing about him was not his size but his angry demeanor. He lunged at me as if he thought he could tackle me. Without think-ing, I turned and shouted, "Run!" I took off like a shot, passing my mother like a cool breeze. Marlene was left to wonder what the heck was going on. Then she instinctively began to run. All the while she shouted, "I don't want to die out here." Her thought was that if she died, her own spirit might encounter the very spirit from which we were running.

Although we were scared out of our wits, we had the presence of mind to take pictures behind us as we ran. Oddly enough, not one picture taken on the battlefield after that encounter came out. Strangely, the pictures we took after we left the field were fine.

Abraham Lincoln Lives on in The White House

Sixteen hundred Pennsylvania Avenue is America's most notable address. Since 1800, The White House has been home to our nation's Presidents and their families. Some former occupants have referred to The White House as cold, drafty, and impossible to heat. Most, however, have said they enjoyed their time there.

Life in The White House has not always gone smoothly. At times it has been downright difficult. For instance, during the War of 1812, British troops set the mansion ablaze. Most of the furnishings became charred ruins. It would be several years before the building would be inhabitable.

The White House is home not only to our country's President, but it is also the residence of numerous ghosts. It has been said there is more action in the house when everyone is asleep than there is during daylight hours. At times it's difficult for White House residents to rest for all the unearthly activity. With all the bumps, knocks, thuds, and creaks, a person could get more sleep in an amusement park.

If the ghosts haunting The White House were alive, they certainly would be on the top of the social registry. The spirits of Abigail Adams, James Garfield, Andrew Jackson, William Henry Harrison, John Tyler, Thomas Jefferson, Mrs. Grover Cleveland, John F. Kennedy, Willie Lincoln, Grace Coolidge, and Dolley Madison have all made at least one appearance in The White House. Eleanor Roosevelt, Mary Todd Lincoln, Ulysses S. Grant, Amy Carter, and Harry Truman have all had an encounter with a White House ghost at one time or another.

The ghost most often encountered is that of Abraham Lincoln. Although the Civil War was over when he was assassinated, Lincoln believed his work was far from complete. It was his intense desire to rebuild the South, thereby reuniting the country on equal terms. Our dedicated sixteenth President is yet another example of a person who died before finishing his mission on earth and who, in spirit, is forever tied to the realm of the living.

Theodore Roosevelt, Benjamin Harrison, Grover Cleveland, Grace Coolidge, Queen Wilhemina of the Netherlands, Harry Truman, Maureen Reagan, Winston Churchill, Ladybird Johnson, and Jacqueline Kennedy have all said Lincoln was in their presence at least once. Dozens of maids, workmen, servants, and statesmen have also reported an encounter with the dead president.

Lincoln, who believed in the supernatural, held séances on a regular basis. All types of psychics visited The White House during his administration. In fact, the clairvoyant President even foretold his own death.

Shortly before his demise, Lincoln witnessed a comet in the night sky. The event convinced him that the end of his life was drawing near. He also predicted he would be elected to a second term but that he would not live to see it end. Sadly, a recurring dream of his own funeral troubled him.

Perhaps it was Lincoln's belief in the paranormal that made it possible for him to spend time on earth as a ghost. Could his subconscious have made it feasible for him to live on in The White House, to oversee the running of his beloved country? Whatever the means for his continued presence, the responsibility he felt for the nation apparently did not end with his death.

Adam Taunton, who worked in security at The White House, says he encountered the Civil War president. "At night, when I made my rounds past the Lincoln bedroom, I sometimes heard footsteps," Taunton explains. "When I opened the door, I could never find anyone there; but right after I closed it, the footsteps began again. This made me determined to find out what was really going on.

"One night I waited by the door until I heard the footsteps. I threw open the door and saw President Lincoln pacing back and forth. His head hung low and his hands were clasped behind his back. When he looked up at me, I closed the door. I don't really know why. I guess I was in shock. A few seconds later, I opened the door, but he was gone."

Taunton never reported the sighting. "I didn't want everyone to think I was crazy, but now that I no longer work at The White House I don't give a damn what anyone thinks."

It is sad to think that the ghost of Abraham Lincoln wanders aimlessly throughout The White House instead of resting in peace. If only he could realize how profoundly his many accomplishments affected society in a positive way, perhaps he could move on to the afterlife with a clear conscience.

Ocean City's Haunted Hotels

Colonel Henry Norwood of Cheltenham, England, was born into privilege in 1615. His father, Henry, was a lawyer who married his late business partner's wife, Elizabeth. Together, they had two children, Thomas and Henry.

As time passed, young Henry grew unhappy with the conflict raging in his homeland. England was facing a national war. Henry decided at the age of thirty-five to leave and sail to America.

Henry Norwood and more than three hundred passengers left England bound for Virginia in September 1649 aboard a ship called *The Virginia Merchant*. Henry was convinced that he had all the supplies necessary to make a safe and successful crossing. But during the journey, they encountered a great storm that almost sank the ship. *The Virginia Merchant* was so badly ripped apart that it was barely able to stay afloat.

The food supply was ruined when the gully of the ship flooded, leaving the passengers nothing to eat but rats. The drinking supply was contaminated with salt water, causing the passengers to become violently ill. They were truly in a desperate situation.

The disabled ship slowly moved in whatever direction the sea chose to carry it. In the early years of ocean voyages, travelers had no knowledge of longitude, and their maps were unreliable to say the least. It was impossible for Henry to predict their exact location.

The battered ship finally reached land in January 1650. It stopped off the coast of what would later become Ocean City, Maryland. Nineteen men and women, including Henry, departed from the ship at what is now 118th Street in Ocean City to search for help. They made their camp there, nestled amid the sand dunes.

Those who stayed onboard *The Virginia Merchant* were on the brink of starvation and eventually turned to cannibalism.

Soon afterward, the ship set sail for Chesapeake Bay. Probably due to lack of nourishment, the crew simply abandoned the search party on the desolate shore of the deserted island. By the time the native Indians found the members of Henry's party, only thirteen remained alive. Five had died from the cold or starvation, and one woman was missing.

The Assateague Indians resided near what is now the town of Berlin, five miles west of Ocean City. On one of their outings to the oceanfront, they happened upon Henry's haggard search party.

The kind Assateagues took the exhausted and desperate new-comers to their camp and gave them food and a warm place to sleep. It wasn't long before members of the group regained their health.

After a couple of weeks, Henry and the others were on their way to civilization. They made it to Virginia on foot, where they found the other passengers. Everyone was accounted for except for the woman lost somewhere on the desolate shore of Ocean City. What happened to her is a mystery.

It's been written that when Norwood's partly left their camp on 118th Street to search for food, six people, including the missing woman, stayed behind. When the party returned, they found five dead and no sign of the woman. They searched the area only to find fragments of her tattered and bloodstained clothing.

Since the woman's body was never recovered, it's believed that she did not die from the cold or starvation but was probably carried off and devoured by wolves. Ocean City had an abundance of wolves during the seventeenth century. There are several accounts of attacks on visitors.

Although the anonymous woman's remains were not found, there are people who believe her spirit has never left Ocean City. Her frightened ghost is said to wander the place where she is thought to have violently lost her life.

People staying in hotels near 118th Street have reported a strange tapping sound on the outside of their window. When they pulled back the curtains, the ghost of a woman was hovering in midair. Her bloodstained face seemed to plead for help.

In the summer of 2000, the Gresham family witnessed this spectacle. "My husband, our two kids, and myself, were fast asleep in our hotel room in north Ocean City," Anne Gresham explains. "We'd been here several times before and never had any trouble.

"Late one night my son, Billy, heard a banging sound on the window. He couldn't imagine what it could be, because we were on the fourteenth floor. He tiptoed over to the window and jerked back the curtains. Then he let out a scream.

"My husband and I jumped out of bed and ran over to him. He was as white as a sheet. He stood there speechless pointing at the window. When we looked out, we couldn't believe what we saw. There was a woman floating outside the ledge! It seems impossible, but it's true. We knew she had to be a ghost. Her clothes were torn, and her face was dripping blood. It was the scariest thing I'd ever seen. We didn't know what to do. We stared back at her for a minute and then she disappeared. I thought we were safe all the way up on the fourteenth floor, but I guess I was wrong."

On rare occasions, the missing woman has been known to take refuge inside local hotel rooms. Last spring, Martha Finny encountered her ghost while attending to one of the vacant rooms. Martha says, "When I came to clean the room, I saw what looked like an imprint of a person on the bed. I thought it was strange, but I decided to ignore it and get on with my chores. I changed the bedding and continued cleaning. When I got ready to leave, I noticed the same imprint on the bed that was there before. I was the only person there, and I know nobody lay on the bed after I made it. I pulled on the bedspread, but it wouldn't smooth out. It looked like somebody was lying there, only I just couldn't see them."

Most people are convinced these unusual occurrences prove that the spirit of the missing woman really does exist. This poor woman's terrifying ordeal seems to have left her ghost restless, trapped in the time of her agonizing death. Her bloody apparition is a sad reminder of the hardships endured by early visitors to our desolate shores.

❧⊙❧

Ocean City is considered young compared to other East Coast communities. Founded in 1875, the city originally was named The Ladies' Resort to the Ocean, which eventually was changed to Ocean City for commercial purposes.

The town's original name was derived from the fact that most of the hotels were owned and managed by women. These women had little help running their establishments. They prepared three meals a day for their guests, washed the bedding by hand, and oversaw all other aspects of running a business. They certainly had their hands full, especially during the height of the tourist season. By the standards of the late nineteenth century, the women of Ocean City were far ahead of their time.

In the early years of the resort community, Ocean City hotels were quite grand. The Atlantic opened its doors in 1875 as the city's first luxury hotel. Others followed, such as the Nordica Hotel, which was not as large as most area hotels but still fashionable. Located at the corner of Talbot Street and the boardwalk, the Nordica was known to exist in 1905. Not much remains of the building except a small portion of its back section.

During its heyday, the Nordica was the scene of an unimaginable tragedy. An opera singer, her identity unknown, met her doom inside the glamorous hotel. She was so despondent that she hung herself from one of the grand chandeliers. After the singer's death, the Nordica became known for its hauntings. Guests were awakened by frightening noises on a regular basis.

Fire struck the Nordica Hotel in 1925, leaving only a small portion of the wooden structure standing. After the fire, it was presumed the spirit of the tortured opera star had vanished with the building. This does not seem to be the case. Some of the businesses that now stand along the boardwalk where the infamous hotel once stood are said to be the sites of supernatural events. Several employees in these haunted businesses have reported spooky experiences.

Timothy Quarters worked in one of the boardwalk businesses many years ago and encountered the ghost of the Nordica Hotel.

"When I was a young man in the 1950s, I was a busboy in a restaurant that was built where the old Nordica used to be," Tim says. "In those days, the bus boys stayed late to wash dishes after the restaurant closed.

"There was one night I worked that was pretty slow. The boss let everybody go home early except me. He was in his office, and I was in the kitchen washing dishes. I heard loud noises coming from the dining hall. I thought it was just the boss stacking chairs. Back then we used to turn the chairs upside down and put them on top of the tables before we left for the night.

"When I was through with the dishes, I went to tell the boss I was leaving. He asked me what all the racket was. I said, 'I thought it was you stacking chairs in the dining hall.' He said he'd been in his office all night. We went to the dining hall, and all the chairs were stacked like they were supposed to be. The boss said that I was a hard worker. I wanted to take the credit for it but I told him the truth—it wasn't me. Then we locked the doors and left.

"The next afternoon when we opened, the boss and I were the first ones there. The chairs were off the tables and scattered all over the room! No one could've done it before we got there, because the boss had the only key. I told him I was too spooked to work there anymore. I finished out the night and never went back."

Young Pricilla Montgomery also worked on the boardwalk. Unlike Timothy Quarters' story, her spirited tale is set in modern times. "Last year I took a summer job in one of the shops on the corner of Talbot Street and the boardwalk," says Pricilla. "One day, we were even more busy than usual. My manager, Joyce, and I took more time counting receipts than we normally did, so by the time we were ready to leave, it was really late. I usually check the bathrooms after closing, but that night I was so busy I forgot.

"We heard a lot of commotion in the front of the shop. I thought it was somebody who'd been in the bathroom trying to get out of the store. When we heard things breaking and crashing to the floor, we realized we were in real danger. We were so scared we decided to hide in Joyce's office and wait for whoever it was to leave.

"When the noise finally stopped, we thought it was probably safe to leave the office. The front of the store was a mess! We looked around, but the store was empty and the door was still locked. Nobody could've gotten out and re-locked the door without a key. It had to have been the Nordica ghost. I'd heard about her from other people who worked around there, but I never thought we'd be in the same store. She was a little too close for comfort if you ask me."

The suicidal singer's despondency might have turned to anger since the time of her death. Her disturbed spirit seems intent on making others as miserable as she. Until her sorrowful soul is finally at peace, those around her will have to suffer the consequences of her obvious discontent.

The Seaman
Who Can't Be Rescued

During the 1950s, clamming became a booming business in Ocean City. Most of the clam beds in the waters off the East Coast had been depleted, except for those off the Delmarva Peninsula. Clammers from up and down the coast flocked to Ocean City to take advantage of the rich beds of huge clams. Those in the community who owned large boats found themselves with highly successful businesses.

To be suitable for clamming, a boat needed to be nearly eighty feet long, and have the capacity to carry heavy dredge equipment. Most Ocean City boat owners found it easy to meet these requirements. Then in the 1970s, the National Marine Fishing Service imposed new regulations and licensing fees for all clamming businesses. Suddenly, clamming was not as lucrative. The high fees and taxes made it necessary for clammers to set sail in inclement weather for added revenue. Ocean City clammers worked in gale winds for an extra day's wage.

Captain Robert Martin was one of those affected by the new licensing laws. He, too, would have to clam in all kinds of weather. Having come from a long line of clammers, he knew the dangers of rough seas and that he needed the sturdiest boat available.

Martin's ship, the Atlantic Mist, had the capability to stay at sea for up to five days. The Atlantic Mist was an all-steel vessel that cost nearly two hundred thousand dollars. With all the time, money, and precision that went into her construction, one might think the Atlantic Mist would have been impervious to the hazards of high seas. But she went down in the waves of a winter storm off the coast of Ocean City in February 1985.

The captain and his three crewmen floated in the frigid ocean for more than ten hours. If not for their wet suits, they would have died from hypothermia in less than an hour. Fellow clammers finally happened upon them. By then, only three men remained alive in the icy sea. One crewman had died hours before the others were rescued. It is believed that the lost clammer did not know how to swim.

Martin and the two surviving crewmen desperately clutched their coworker's body until help arrived. They risked their lives on that dark night to keep their friend's remains from being lost to the sea forever.

Since the accident, a sad spectacle has been witnessed periodically in the waters of Ocean City. Reports of a man in a wet suit waving frantically for help have sent lifeguards rushing to the scene, only to find no one there. A lifeguard named Jack Reddy had an encounter with the drowning apparition in the spring of 1997. "I remember the beach wasn't very crowded that day," Jack says. "That's probably because the water was still cold.

"We go through a lot of training to be a lifeguard in Ocean City, so I know what to look for. I know exactly what to do in an emergency situation. I've had CPR training and every other kind of training needed to make a successful rescue. Anyone off the street can't be a lifeguard; you have to be an excellent swimmer, too.

"The morning I saw the guy drowning was real clear. But even if it weren't, I would've been able to see him. I have excellent vision. Forgive me if I sound a little defensive, but I've gotten a lot of grief from people when I tell them this story. Some people have even laughed in my face.

"Anyway, that morning I saw a man in the water wildly waving his arms in the air. It was obvious he was in real trouble. He was even close enough for me to hear him screaming. I dove into the water and swam over to where I'd seen him just a few seconds before. He was gone, so I kept diving to try and find him. Believe me—I combed the area, and he was nowhere around.

"I was exhausted by the time I got back to the beach. I don't think I could've swam one more foot. I'd spent at least forty-five minutes in the water looking for the guy. About two hours later, I saw the same man in the water! He couldn't have been more than fifty yards off shore. He was screaming and waving for help. I thought to myself, " Here we go again." I dove in and went to where he was, but, guess what—he wasn't there. I was so determined to find him that I would've done anything. I stayed out there for at least an hour this time.

"When I got back to the beach and settled down, I got to thinking about the whole thing. Then it dawned on me. How could this guy have been in the water for two hours between the times I went out to get him? That would've been a total of almost four hours that he'd spent out there. There's no way anybody, I don't care who he is, could've been out there all that time, especially if he couldn't swim. It's just impossible! I know he didn't come out of the water the whole time I was there, because I was watching and I was there all day. I looked for him from the moment I first saw him until I left in the evening. I'm telling you, this guy wasn't human."

Is it possible the spirit of the drowned clammer has remained off the shore of Ocean City for the past fifteen years? How disturbing that he has been in a state of absolute panic all this time. Overwhelmed by fear and afraid of death, the ghostly clammer seems to be suspended in the moment of his greatest struggle—the fight for life.

The Legend of Zippy Lewis

Zipporah (Zippy) Lewis is one of Ocean City's most memorable characters. She is believed to have been born in Delaware in 1813. Records show that she lived in Ocean City from the early 1830s until her death in 1878. The locals considered her a bit strange because of the way she made her living. She spent her days searching the oceanfront for anything of value that had washed up on shore.

When Zippy was a young woman of sixteen, she married the man of her dreams and had the first of five children. The family was extremely poor but happy. They ate seaweed and whatever else they could pull from the ocean. Zippy's husband built their home out of ship wreckage and driftwood they'd found along the beach. Their unusual shack stood somewhere near 117th Street, but the exact location is not known.

In the mid-1850s, Zippy's life took a tragic turn. Her husband left on an ocean voyage and never returned. Zippy's heart was broken. Every day she walked to the highest sand dune and looked out over the ocean, searching for any sign of her missing husband. After several years, Zippy realized that he was never coming back.

Zippy's daily trips to the beach turned out to be her salvation. Rumor has it that she found hundreds of Spanish coins that had washed up on shore and that she later sold them for a great deal of money. With her newfound wealth, she bought several large parcels of land. In spite of her monetary gain, she continued to live a meager existence. She furnished her small shack entirely with items she had salvaged from sunken ships.

All day, every day, Zippy searched the oceanfront for "beach money." No matter how high the temperature, she wore a long black dress that covered every inch of her body. Her shawl dragged along the sand as she walked stooped over for hours on end. Her sunbonnet covered much of her rugged face, but there was no mistaking Zippy Lewis. Her odd presence was a common sight in Ocean City.

In one instance, Zippy sat for more than twelve hours on a sea chest she'd found. She was afraid that if she left it unguarded the county would claim it. Since it was too heavy to lift by herself, she waited until dark and then went for help.

Over the years, Zippy accumulated a small fortune in coins. Legend has it that she buried them near her home, along with other sea treasures. Because of her instinct for knowing exactly where to find valuable salvage, she became known as the local "seeress." This is a person who is able to predict future events.

Zippy's death was even more tragic than the loss of her beloved husband. It is believed that she burned to death inside her home. Some people think she fell into the fireplace, causing her clothes to catch fire. This was indeed a sad end to an extraordinary life.

In her will, Zippy left all her property to her two daughters, Mary and Jinsey. She left her two remaining sons, Jonathan and George, only one dollar each. Records show that her eldest son, Jacob, had already died by that time.

Zippy carried less than five dollars when she died. The whereabouts of her treasure went with her to the grave. If Mary and Jinsey had kept the land they inherited from their mother, their descendants would have been millionaires. In her lifetime, Zippy had accumulated more than twenty blocks of prime Ocean City real estate.

Mystery surrounds the remains of Zippy Lewis. Her gravesite has never been found. Her body and her treasure are presumed to lie somewhere near the site of her former home. Treasure hunters have searched the area for years, but no one has ever found so much as one coin of Zippy's fortune.

One might think Zippy's painful death would be the end of her remarkable story. But her ghost is said to remain on the beaches of Ocean City. Her spirit is often seen wearing the long black dress for which she was so famous in life.

Frank Howell of Baltimore claims to have come face to face with Zippy's ghost during a visit to Ocean City in July 1999. "I was walking the beach early that morning when I passed a peculiar-looking woman," Frank says. "She was on her hands and knees, sifting through the sand. Her back was bowed, like she'd spent a lot of time stooped over. It was already very hot, so I thought it was strange that she was totally covered by a heavy black dress.

"I thought she'd lost something in the sand, so I asked her if she needed any help, but she just ignored me. I walked a few feet, then turned to take one last look at her, but she was gone. She'd simply disappeared!"

Zippy's ghost can also be seen sitting patiently on a sea chest in the sweltering summer sun. Her arms are folded and her face wears a look of determination. It may be that she stubbornly refuses to let death cheat her out of one of her most cherished finds.

Although Zippy died more than one hundred twenty years ago, there's no question that her ghost continues to hunt ocean treasure. She walks back and forth along the beach, relentlessly searching for her next big find. Perhaps if you walk the beach in the early morning hours as Frank Howell did, you may catch a glimpse of Zippy Lewis hunched over, sifting through the sand.

Watch Out for Men in Uniform

When the Japanese bombed Pearl Harbor, the country soon learned of the tragic loss of American lives in the attack. What was not commonly known was that during the winter of 1942, German submarines regularly patrolled the waters off the coast of Ocean City. They lay in wait for virtually any enemy vessel to cross their paths, whether it be civilian or military. Several allied ships met their doom in Maryland's waters when confronted by German U-boats.

February 1942 turned out to be a deadly month for allied ships off the Delmarva Peninsula. The tankers W.L. Steed, Indian Arrow, and the China Arrow and the freighter Olinda were destroyed by German U-boats.

The Germans' most deadly conquest of that February was the sinking of the destroyer U.S.S. Jacob Jones. More than one hundred courageous seamen lost their lives when the Jones was torpedoed and sank beneath the waters off Ocean City's shore.

One of the most somber memories of older Ocean City residents is the sinking of the American ship David Atwater on April 2, 1942. After the Germans sank the Atwater, they opened fire on those who managed to board the lifeboats. They callously machine-gunned the helpless Americans as they tried to make it to shore. Only three of thirty-one men survived the attack. Several of their bullet-riddled bodies later washed up on the city's beaches.

Blackouts became mandatory in the resort community during the summer of 1942. This was done to keep passing vessels from being caught in the glow of city lights and becoming easy targets for German gunboats. Merchant ship captains traveling off the coast of Ocean City were so frightened of an enemy attack that they often steered too close to the shoreline, grounding their ships in the shallow waters.

During the time the U-boats inhabited Ocean City waters, foot guardsmen and attack dogs patrolled the beaches regularly. Foxholes were dug in sand dunes to allow guards to keep a watchful eye on enemy activities. For a short while, it seemed as if the community had been transformed into a military base.

The blackouts continued until the summer of 1943, when the fear of looming German submarines subsided. After the threat of enemy forces had passed, Ocean City returned to a peaceful vacation destination. Visitors found the place as placid as they always had—with one exception. The ghosts of slaughtered seamen were believed to remain in Ocean City. Sightings were reported almost immediately after their horrific deaths.

Today, ample evidence suggests that some of the lost sailors still call Ocean City home. People working in local businesses witness their curious apparitions regularly. Kathy Crain claims that at least one of these spirits is a peeping Tom. "I work in a store at the Gold Coast Mall on 117th Street," Kathy says. "When business is slow, I sometimes leave my register to use the restroom.

"One afternoon while I was washing my hands, I saw a face looking back at me from the mirror, and it wasn't mine! It was just a face with no body! I looked behind me to see whose reflection it was, but nobody was there. I looked back at the mirror, and there he was— staring at me. It makes me wonder just how long he had been watching me.

"He was a young guy with real short blond hair. He was wearing some sort of uniform, only I don't know what kind it was. His eyes were baby blue. I thought he was cute, as cute as a ghost can be, anyway.

"Normally, if I saw a ghost I'd be scared to death. But this time I was more angry than scared. Dead or alive, he should know that it's not polite to watch a woman while she's in the restroom."

Sadness Hovers over St. Paul's Cemetery

In 1823 Berlin, Maryland, was a small village with two stores and eighteen houses. As it became known as a good place to raise a family and run a business, the population grew to nearly three hundred in just a couple of years. There was one problem, however: Berlin did not have a church within a five-mile radius. Townspeople traveled several miles to attend Sunday services at Old St. Martin's Church. The solution was to build a church in the center of town.

St. Paul's Episcopal Church was built in 1825, facing what is now called Church Street. Residents were thrilled to have such a grand church within walking distance. As Berlin grew, so did the church cemetery. Before long, St. Paul's Cemetery took up almost an entire city block.

Unfortunately, the neighborhood church was unable to pass through the decades unscathed. In the fall of 1904, a devastating fire broke out during a northeaster. It was the third fire in less than ten years to nearly destroy Berlin. Flames completely gutted St. Paul's Church, leaving only its thick outer walls standing. The church did not reopen until three years after the blaze.

After St. Paul's was reconstructed, it took on an entirely different appearance. Its new interior resembled a medieval cathedral. The exterior was done in Romanesque Revival style, which was popular at the time. It featured large rounded sanctuary windows and a tall arched doorway.

Today the church has a fresh coat of white paint covering its ancient brick walls. A bright red door complements the building beautifully. The pristine condition of both church and cemetery make it hard to guess their age. Nevertheless, one grim reminder of the past lingers behind the church on a nearby nature trail.

On moonlit nights, the ghost of a lovely young woman hovers above the small pond on the Stephen Decatur Nature Trail. Her slender figure has startled countless visitors through the years.

Katrina Doyle, along with her boyfriend, Ted, stumbled upon the image of the woman one summer during a romantic stroll on the trail. "Ted and I both live with our parents, so we usually need to go out to get any privacy," Katrina says. "We spend a lot of time walking the nature trail. We were down at the pond on the night we saw the ghost. I was sitting on the ground feeding the ducks when Ted started tapping on me. He never said a word—he just stood there poking me on the back of my head. Then I looked up and saw why he was speechless.

"There was a beautiful woman floating over the pond! I mean she was really gorgeous. I blinked a few times to make sure I wasn't seeing things. She was real! She was actually floating in the air above the pond. The moon was full, so I saw her really clearly. The ghost looked so sad that I immediately felt sorry for her. I wasn't afraid, because she seemed so delicate and frail. When our eyes met, I could feel her pain. I could tell she'd lost somebody she really loved. Don't ask me how, I could just tell.

"She was wearing a long, yellow dress with lace trim. It looked like a turn-of-the-century dress—the twentieth century, I mean, not the twenty-first. The sleeves were puffed, and the waist was cut tight to her body. Her clothes looked so uncomfortable. I can't image ever having to wear something like that.

"I noticed she had a flower in her hands. After we lost eye contact, she lowered her head and slowly faded away. After she was gone, I saw the flower floating in the pond."

The dazzling apparition can be spotted in St. Paul's Cemetery, as well as on the nature trail. Although most sightings are on the trail, she appears from time to time on the grounds where her body is believed buried.

William Randle had a brief encounter with her in the fall of 1999 while driving on Tripoli Street beside St. Paul's Cemetery. "I saw her in the headlights of my car," William says. "She was so beautiful that

I slowed down to get a better look at her. She was dressed so old-fashioned. Everything about her was mysterious.

"I wondered what she was doing all alone in a graveyard at that time of night. I didn't think it was safe for her to be there, so I rolled down my car window to see if she needed a lift anywhere. When I called to her, she turned and faced me. Then she started to rise straight up in the air. It was amazing! Before I knew it, she was gone. She just disappeared."

Who was this beautiful woman?. Why is she so unhappy, and why does she walk the grounds near where her body rests? Perhaps she searches for a lost loved one, as Katrina Doyle believes. For whatever the reason, the mysterious specter does not appear to be ready to leave any time soon. Sightings of her seem to be steadily on the rise.

The Stephen Decatur Nature Trail is known to harbor supernatural beings such as this one.

Mean Joe Morgue
Haunts Church Circle

Church Circle in Annapolis, Maryland, was designed more than three centuries ago. St. Anne's Church, which is enclosed by Church Circle, is the third church to stand on the property. The first church became too small for the growing population of Annapolis, so a larger church was built. The second church was destroyed by fire, which led to the creation of the elegant church standing today.

Inside Church Circle lie the bodies of several prominent citizens. However, the body of the most colorful person associated with St. Anne's is buried elsewhere. His name was Joseph Simmons, and he was sexton of the church for almost seventy years. He died in 1836 at the age of one hundred.

Simmons was not commonly known by his given name. He was called Joe Morgue because of his longtime obsession with grave digging. It was a hobby he took very seriously. He was known to spend a great deal of time digging in the ground around the church. Some say he enjoyed digging up coffins.

Townspeople considered Joe Morgue eccentric. He was not particularly well liked because of his gruff and odd demeanor. He wore torn, dirty clothing and let his hair grow long and unkempt. When children teased him about his strange appearance, he was known to say, "I'll have you someday." This statement was thought to mean that someday he would be digging a grave for them.

When a man named Jeffrey Jig had fallen into a deep coma, people thought he was dead and prepared his body for burial. As Joe Morgue threw dirt onto the coffin, a fierce pounding came from inside the grave. Joe Morgue didn't let that stop him. He continued to throw dirt over the coffin. Finally, the townspeople forced the strange gravedigger to stop. Joe was furious! He said, "He's got to die sometime, and if he's not dead, he ought to be."

After Joe Morgue's death, the people of Annapolis thought they had seen the last of the unpopular sexton. But since the middle of the nineteenth century, Joe's ghost has been seen on several occasions inside Church Circle.

One witness is David Doppler. "When I was walking past Church Circle one evening, I heard the sound of what I thought was digging. I could tell, because the scraping of the shovel against the ground made a very distinctive noise. I felt compelled to investigate, so I walked toward the scraping sound," he recalls.

"When I rounded the corner of the church, I saw a dirty, long-haired man standing on top of one of the graves. He had a shovel in his hands. When he saw me, he shook his shovel and shouted obscenities at me. I thought he was a nut! Then he vanished right before my eyes. Truthfully, after seeing him disappear, I thought I must be the nut. I promise you, that's the last time I'll ever investigate a strange noise."

Others claim to have seen the ghost of Joe Morgue as well. He's been known to startle visitors by popping out in front of them as they pass through the property. A group of frightened children swore that his ghost actually chased them out of Church Circle. He has also been seen inside the church, sitting in one of the pews.

If you visit Church Circle after dark, perhaps Joe will show himself to you. Be prepared, for he's not a very hospitable host. For him, grave digging is a solitary pastime.

The Accident-Prone Men of Annapolis

The stately Government House in Annapolis was constructed shortly after the Civil War as a residence for Maryland's governors. The large brick home was originally built in the Victorian style but has since undergone extensive remodeling. Several additions were made in the 1930s, which changed its appearance dramatically.

Throughout the years, the Government House has hosted Maryland's most prominent citizens, including an accomplished attorney named Reverdy Johnson. Johnson had served in the United States Senate for several years, and at one time served as Maryland's attorney general. He also served as the country's minister to England. Needless to say, Johnson was highly respected by the citizens of Annapolis.

In February 1876, a state dinner was given at the Government House for all of Maryland's political leaders. Johnson was among those invited, of course.

As the party got underway, the mansion filled with music and laughter. Champagne flowed like water, and guests feasted on the best cuts of beef and sumptuous desserts. No expense was spared in making this dinner the grandest of the season. But the wonderful food and drink weren't the reason this party would never be forgotten.

As the liquor flowed, the crowd grew louder and the party spread from the mansion onto the lawn. The elegant dinner turned into a rowdy affair in which political discussions grew into heated debates. In all the activity, no one could have guessed the tragedy that was about to take place.

As Reverdy Johnson made his way out the front door, he tripped and fell off the porch. He was obviously seriously injured. Every attempt to save him proved unsuccessful. Guests stood stunned as word spread of Johnson's death. The dining hall quieted, and the festive sounds on the lawn turned to cries of sadness. Though Johnson's life ended that night, the party is said to continue on the lawn of the mansion to this day.

Maryanne Arthur, a domestic worker employed at Government House several years ago, says she witnessed the continuation of the long-ago party on two separate occasions. "One day, while I was working upstairs, I heard voices and old music coming from the dining hall. I thought this was strange because I was the only one in the house. When I ran downstairs, the sounds were gone. Nobody was there. It was just too creepy."

Maryanne's second ghostly encounter took place as she was cleaning the windows on the second floor one day. She explains, "From the window, I saw a lot of people on the front lawn. They were dressed in old-fashioned clothing. I was a little upset, because no one told me there was gonna be a party that day. Anyway, I went downstairs to see if there was something I could do to help out. When I opened the front door, the lawn was empty. There were no signs of any party. From that day on, I minded my own business no matter what I heard."

Other Annapolis residents are known to have witnessed the mysterious party of 1876. While passing in front of Government House, people have heard the faint sounds of music and laughter. On rare occasions, figures dressed in nineteenth-century clothing are seen gathered together on the lawn. Several passersby have even observed the transparent ghost of Reverdy Johnson on the porch where he fell to his death. He sits in a chair with a drink clutched tightly in his hand.

The Government House is not the only place in Annapolis where a deadly accident has taken place. The State House is home to an accident victim as well.

Maryland's State House is the oldest state house still in use in the country. Countless historic events have taken place there throughout the years. It was in this State House in December 1783 that George Washington resigned his commission as commander in chief of the Continental Army. In 1784, the Treaty of Paris was signed within its walls, formally ending the Revolutionary War. For a brief period it even served as our nation's capitol building.

Plans to build the grand State House were conceived in 1696. However, as we all know, sometimes things don't go as planned. It seems the construction of the State House was doomed from the beginning, as if the project had been jinxed.

Soon after the first State House was built, a bolt of lightning struck it. Seven years later, fire completely consumed the building. The second State House fell into such a state of disrepair it had to be torn down and replaced with a third building.

In 1775, a hurricane severely damaged the third State House, and several other minor disasters delayed its completion. Nonetheless, the unfinished building was used for state offices. Finally, in 1792 its construction began once again. This time, it was not the building that met with a horrible fate.

Thomas Dance was the plasterer in charge of repairing the building's grand dome. He worked from sunup until sundown every day except Sunday. Dance took great pride in his work and saw every detail to perfection.

As the completion date approached, Dance looked forward to showing off his fine work. Sadly, he did not live to reap the rewards of his masterpiece. As he put the finishing touches on the dome, he fell to his death.

The State House is thought to be haunted by the frustrated ghost of Thomas Dance. Employees have described sudden gusts of wind through the hallways and cold spots in vacant rooms. Others have spoken of footsteps echoing from empty corridors. In 1997, a group from Washington, D.C., was touring the State House when they apparently angered Dance's spirit. Randy Michaels was the leader of that tour.

"As we were viewing the dome, one of the people on my tour commented that she wasn't impressed with the work," Randy explains. "Suddenly, a bone-chilling gust of wind blew open the doors and rattled the chandeliers above us. This could've been explained if it hadn't happened in July, with the temperature outside in the high nineties."

While visiting Maryland's grand State House, it is advisable to say only good things about Thomas Dance's handiwork. Otherwise, you just might encounter the wrath of the eighteenth-century plasterer for yourself.

Annapolis' Homes Harbor Ghosts of All Kinds

The Brooksby-Shaw House on State Circle in Annapolis is thought to have been built in 1722 for Cornelius Brooksby. Brooksby was truly excited about moving into his new home with his beloved wife. Unfortunately, he died two years before completion of the building. Legend has it that Brooksby's ghost moved into the house to remain beside his one true love in life. He was not about to let death ruin his happiness. Soon after the move, however, the unthinkable happened. Mrs. Brooksby married Thomas Gough.

Gough moved into the house to live with his new bride. As you can imagine, this angered Cornelius Brooksby's spirit beyond belief. Shortly after the Goughs married, unusual things began to happen inside the home. The spirit of the dead husband did whatever he could to make life miserable for the newlyweds. It seems he could not rest in peace for the rage burning inside him. His heavy footsteps were heard in the early-morning hours as if he were pacing back and forth on the second floor. The sound of breaking glass and a man's angry voice woke the couple several times a night.

As time passed, the haunting of the Brooksby-Shaw house intensified. The spirit was not content with merely disturbing the couple's rest. He wanted to make certain the Goughs knew of his deep anger. He began appearing to the newlyweds during the night. His misty figure showed up at the foot of the bed on several occasions and was observed on the staircase and elsewhere on the grounds.

Even after the Goughs moved out of the house, the haunting continued. In the mid-1700s, Cornelius Brooksby's granddaughter Mary and her husband, Sewell Long, moved into the house to begin their life together. Although Mary was Cornelius' relative, his ghost frequently appeared to frighten her and her husband. The bitter spirit is said to have hated all married couples who chose to live under his roof.

Although the building serves as government office space today, many of its features are original, such as the spiral staircase, the woodwork on the second-floor, several door frames, and a supernatural presence from the colonial era.

Disembodied footsteps and a man's angry voice continue to be overheard by witnesses. At times, Cornelius Brooksby's face can be seen peering from a second-floor window. Perhaps he searches for his wife, who left with another man more than two centuries ago.

The Brice House on East Street is also known for its ghosts. In fact, it's presumed to be the most haunted building in all of Annapolis. The wealthy John Brice began construction of the home in the 1740s. Brice died soon after the foundations were laid. He left the property to his son, James, who had the thirty-three-room brick mansion completed.

An accomplished man, James Brice served as mayor of Annapolis for many years, was a member of the governor's council, and was named acting governor of the state. During the Revolution he served as a colonel in the Maryland militia.

James Brice died in 1801; however, it's believed he loved his magnificent home so much, that he simply refused to leave it after death. Since the early nineteenth century, his ghost has been witnessed walking the halls of Brice House. Others have reported seeing his glowing silhouette roaming the grounds. He is also known to stroll East Street for his nightly walks. In fact, James' spirit is the most frequently seen ghost in Annapolis.

The colonel's spirit is not the only one known to dwell inside Brice House. A beautiful young woman is often seen peering from a parlor window. No one knows who this mysterious spirit may have been or why she lingers there. We do know by her clothes that she was a woman of the eighteenth century. She wears an elegant green floor-length dress with detailed embroidery, and her red hair is meticulously fixed atop her head. She was obviously of the gentry, or upper class.

The ghost of a woman who lived among the working class, or commoners as they were called in the eighteenth century, also haunts Brice House. Wearing the clothing of a housemaid, she walks briskly throughout the house, apparently continuing the duties she performed in life. Her eyes are transfixed in a dazed stare. She seems to pay no attention to what goes on around her. As in the case of the elegant colonial woman, no one knows the identity of this ghost or why her soul lingers in the house.

One ghost is thought to welcome visitors to an Annapolis home. This considerate spirit is believed to dwell in the Jonas Green House on Charles Street.

Today the Jonas Green House now serves as an elegant bed and breakfast. One of the oldest buildings in Annapolis, its kitchen and some other sections date back to the 1690s. The beautiful brick-and-shingle facade blends nicely with the colonial atmosphere of the neighborhood.

Not long ago, a fascinating discovery took place inside the Jonas Green House. During the course of restoration work on the home, two colonial shoes, a ledger book dating back to the American Revolution, and other writings from the nineteenth century were found inside a wall. They are now displayed for overnight guests to see. Many portions of the original house remain, including the wooden floors. Green's descendants continue to live there to this very day.

Jonas Green brought his new bride, Anne Catherine, to his home after they married in May 1738. Green was a printer, and a distant cousin of Benjamin Franklin. He ran the Maryland Gazette newspaper and became the official printer of the colony. Portions of the printing shop were discovered in the backyard of the house, where they remain today. Green was so well liked that when he died in 1767, the entire town grieved.

Anne was truly an amazing woman. Her husband died, leaving her to pay his large debts. She not only found a way to clear his accounts, but also won a printing contract with the legislature in her own name—a difficult task for an eighteenth-century woman. Later, Anne raised enough money to buy three more properties in Annapolis. She also operated and expanded the circulation of the Gazette. She even made chocolate, which she sold at the City Dock.

In the span of twenty-two years, Anne gave birth to fourteen children in the Jonas Green House. She was a good mother and loved each child dearly. Not unusual for the times, six of her children died in the home before they reached the age of six. Anne died at the age of sixty in 1775. Her spirit and the spirit of at least one of her children are believed to remain inside the home.

Several years ago, while a descendant of Jonas Green stayed in the bedroom above the kitchen, he awoke to the sound of a child crying. As his eyes adjusted to the darkness, he could see the ghost of a little girl in the corner of the room. Since then, this sad little spirit has been frequently seen and heard. On rare occasions, a woman's cries emanate from the second floor. Perhaps it's Anne's ghost, distraught over the death of yet another child.

Other odd occurrences take place within the Jonas Green House. Locked doors are found unlocked. Voices and footsteps are sometimes heard in the night; resident dogs are sometimes "spooked" for no apparent reason; while passing a room, visitors often observe someone out of the corner of their eye, only to see the figure vanish a moment later.

One of the home's owners recently experienced an unexplainable event while alone there. "The house has an excellent security system that flashes green if a door or window is left open. When they are closed, it shows a steady green light," she explains.

"One afternoon, I was reading a book in full view of the security system. I was sure the light was a solid green. Suddenly, the light began to flash. I felt a draft coming from the other side of the house. When I got up and looked around, I found a locked door had somehow opened. These kinds of things happen all the time."

In spite of the hauntings, the feeling in the house overall is friendly and peaceful. Guests consider themselves lucky to spend the night. This same owner believes this is because Anne's ghost is happy to have a family living in her home once again. Whatever the reason, the spirit inside the Jonas Green House seems to welcome visitors with open arms.

The Jonas Green House is a private residence. If you'd like to view the artifacts found in the home, you'll have to make arrangements to spend the night. It is definitely worth visiting!

The Guardian Angel
of Wilmington

S ome spirits actually protect the people around them. They literally roam the earth doing good deeds for those in need. An extraordinary example took place in Wilmington, Delaware.

Several years ago, Wilmington experienced an unusually heavy snowstorm. This rare event upset Thomas Chambers greatly. He lived several miles outside town and thought the blizzard might keep him from getting to work.

Chambers was a conscientious employee who bragged that he had only missed four days of work in ten years. He was not about to let this freak storm keep him from his job. He decided to leave home several hours before daylight, allowing plenty of time to reach his place of employment. Along the way, his car skidded off the road into an icy ditch. Try as he might, he could not get his vehicle back on the road. He found himself stranded far from both home and work. Though ill dressed for a walk in the snow, he knew his only chance for survival was to leave the safety of his car and look for help on foot.

The going was rough. Chambers began to lose all hope of finding shelter and he wondered whether he would make it out of the storm alive. The feeling left his hands and feet, but he continued to trudge along with only the streetlights to guide him.

Suddenly the walk became easier. It wasn't because the snow stopped falling or that the temperature had risen. Chambers wondered what could possibly be helping him get through this life-threatening ordeal. A moment later he got his answer. When he reached the next streetlight, he saw not only his shadow on the snow but, much to his surprise, a second shadowy figure. It looked as if he were walking with someone.

Unbelievably, he wasn't scared. He realized that the mysterious apparition was somehow helping him survive. They continued to walk together for several more miles. When he finally arrived at work, Chambers was neither cold nor tired, and his clothing was warm and dry. He credits his invisible friend for saving his life.

Is it possible that the caring people of the world exist as angels after their lives end? Many people feel this is the case. Just ask Thomas Chambers.

Colonial Life Continues at Mount Vernon

Mount Vernon, George Washington's beloved home, is situated fifteen miles south of Washington, D.C. The twenty-room mansion overlooks the sparkling waters of the Potomac River in northern Virginia. Thanks to its loving caretakers, Mount Vernon remains as beautiful today as it was during the former President's lifetime, if not more so.

The estate's eight thousand acres are meticulously maintained, and the mansion's furnishings are as they were during the eighteenth century. The great man's possessions are placed throughout the magnificent home, and an on-site museum houses Washington family memorabilia.

Washington owned Mount Vernon for almost half a century, during which time he added several rooms. When called upon to be our country's first President in 1789, Washington was reluctant to leave the estate. His happiest moments were spent toiling in the lush gardens of Mount Vernon's landscape. However, the intense responsibility he felt for our young country drove him from his favorite place on earth. Washington died in 1799 having spent just two peaceful years at Mount Vernon after his two terms as President ended.

During the last years Washington spent at Mount Vernon, friends and family continuously surrounded him. Spending time with his grandchildren, his wife, and well-wishers was extremely important to the American hero.

Those wonderful days at Mount Vernon were the happiest of Washington's eventful life. Knowing this, it is not surprising to hear stories of the great man's ghost wandering the corridors of his former home. Washington's apparition is most often seen in the pine-paneled study where he spent a great number of early-morning and late-night hours.

A former employee of the mansion, Rebecca Starbridge, claims to have had a face-to-face encounter with the dead President. "Before I'd leave for the evening, I always checked to see if anyone was in the rooms. One night something so scary happened that I'll never forget it. That night, when I looked inside the study, I saw George Washington's ghost sitting in a chair behind the desk. I could actually see right through him! He was busy writing something with a quill pen. It took him over a minute to notice me standing in the doorway.

"When he finally looked up and saw me, he motioned for me to come in. I took a couple of steps toward him, but he just faded away. I've heard a lot of people around here say they've seen the ghost of President Washington, but I never thought I'd be one of them."

It seems Mount Vernon is but one of many places to harbor the spirit of George Washington. He has also been witnessed in Annapolis, Gettysburg, Valley Forge, Philadelphia, and Williamsburg, just to name a few.

Washington isn't the only ghost at Mount Vernon. The spirits of Martha Washington and her daughter, Patsy Custis, are often witnessed in the drawing room. The ghost of an unknown field worker has made several appearances in the colonial gardens of the estate.

During extended leaves from Mount Vernon, Washington wrote letters to his overseers, demanding the gardens be kept in top form. Even after battle, his thoughts returned to the lavish grounds of his estate. Those who managed the gardens felt intense pressure to do as they were told. It may be for this reason that a ghostly farmhand continues with his tedious duties centuries after his death.

Several years ago, Brian Hendricks, who worked in the Mount Vernon gardens, looked behind him to see the spirit of this diligent gardener. "I was the first one on the grounds that morning," Brian explains. "I started work as usual, then a minute later I heard someone behind me. When I turned to see who it was, I saw a man working about thirty yards away. I couldn't make him out clearly, because he was so dark. He was standing in the bright sunlight but he was completely shaded, like he was covered with gray paint.

"He started digging in the dirt, so I shouted for him to stop. I thought he was going to destroy the gardens. I hollered at him several more times, but he just wouldn't stop digging. I thought I was going to have to physically make him stop, so I ran toward him.

"I know this sounds strange, but when I got within five yards of him, he vanished; when I got to where he'd been standing, everything was fine, "Hendricks says. "He hadn't moved as much as one granule of dirt. I don't know what it was I saw that day, but I know it wasn't of this earth."

Does one of George Washington's field hands continue with the work he did so conscientiously during his lifetime? If you ask Brian Hendricks, the answer to this question is an emphatic "You bet!"

An Angry Spirit Dwells in the Custom House

The Custom House was the center of activity in the bustling colonial city of Yorktown, Virginia. Early in the eighteenth century, seafaring merchants were required to pay taxes and register their goods at this busy building on Main Street. At that time, Richard Ambler was collector of ports and owner of the Custom House. He was known for spreading rumors that caused scandal throughout the colonies.

Shippers halfway around the world repeated Ambler's outlandish stories. Although he had been reprimanded on several occasions for his irresponsible behavior, he continued telling his troublesome tales. For the most part, the rumors did little real harm until he targeted Virginia Governor Alexander Spottswood.

Ambler believed Spottswood misappropriated funds when he built the outrageously expensive Governor's Palace in Williamsburg. The governor was known for extravagant spending, often showering himself in luxury to the point of treason. Outraged by Spottswood's self-indulgence and the lack of protection he offered sailing vessels from pirates, the citizens of Virginia grew more and more unhappy with their leader.

To make amends, Spottswood sent out a floating search party for the pirate leader known as Blackbeard. The hunt was successful. In November 1718, the murderous marauder was found and killed. His head was cut off and brought to Virginia as proof of his death. Unfortunately, several of the governor's men also died in the fight, one of which was John Ames, who worked alongside Richard Ambler in the Custom House.

Despite the loss of the seafaring heroes, Spottswood was widely acclaimed for taking action against the most feared man of the sea.

He had not only saved hundreds of lives, but also endured great monetary loss, since he financed the endeavor personally. Because of this, Spottswood regained his popularity with the people of Virginia, if only for a short while.

Although saddened by the death of one of their townspeople, the citizens of Yorktown celebrated Blackbeard's demise. Even though the governor's reputation had been restored, Richard Ambler continued to voice his disapproval of him. Ambler's anger grew to a fevered pitch after losing his close friend and coworker. The bitterness Ambler harbored for the colonial leader lasted until his death in 1766, even though the governor had died twenty-six years earlier.

Since those eventful times, countless people have used the Custom House for various purposes. In 1924 the building was purchased by the Daughters of the American Revolution and totally renovated. A charter member of the D.A.R., Alice Drake, wrote of the unusual experience that she had while alone inside the landmark.

In September 1930, Drake wrote the following to a family member: "Late last evening, as I was working in the Custom House, the lights began to flicker; then a minute later, they went out completely. At that moment, I heard a scraping sound coming from the top of the stairs. It was as if something was being dragged across the floor. Even though it was difficult to see, I decided to find out what was making the noise.

"As I crept up the staircase, the sound suddenly stopped. At the top of the stairs was a light, a flickering light, as if a candle was burning. Then, moments later, it went out, leaving me in total darkness. As I found my way down the stairs, the scraping began once again. I ran for the door and never returned!"

Could the strength of his anger be keeping the spirit of Richard Ambler inside the Custom House? His bitterness over John Ames' death may be confining him to the building in which he worked beside his friend for so much of his lifetime. If Ambler's ghost could bring himself to let go of the past, he might move on peacefully.

The Civil War Ghosts of Williamsburg

Battlefields seem to be popular environments for ghosts. And our country has no short supply of places where brave men have laid down their lives for a cause.

It is thought that hundreds of Confederate soldiers believed in their cause so deeply that they simply refuse to give up even in death. They wander the grounds of their demise convinced that someday they shall return to fight. In many cases, soldiers died so quickly and violently that they remain unaware of their own untimely deaths. To them, today is the eve of battle and will always remain so.

One Civil War battle in particular is believed to have left an abundance of ghosts. It was the Battle of Williamsburg, fought on May 5, 1862. On that day, nearly forty thousand soldiers battled hand to hand on the muddy streets of Williamsburg, Virginia, and in the surrounding woods. Almost forty thousand men were killed and thousands more wounded.

During the fight, both the Union and Confederate Armies became lost in the confusion. Thick underbrush quickly filled with the dead and wounded. Lack of visibility due to torrential rainfall and the lack of ammunition added to the fury of the fight. Troops grew tired and discouraged. Not knowing whether friend or foe approached, the men fumbled through the woods of Williamsburg, engaged in more than ten long hours of combat.

Union forces emerged victorious. However, several Confederates refused to acknowledge the loss. For three years, the Federal Army controlled Williamsburg. All the while, Confederate raiders swept silently into town after nightfall to kill all the Union men they could find. In the morning, the townspeople would find the Federals' naked, lifeless bodies on the streets.

It is believed by many that the angry spirits of the men killed in the fight continue to walk the grounds in and around town. Confederate ghosts are witnessed on a regular basis, especially in area hotels. More than a few people have checked out of their lodging houses because an unwelcome apparition occupied their rooms.

Ghosts from the Battle of Williamsburg are known to remain for a variety of reasons. Some stay to be with those who were killed with them. Others are simply afraid of what awaits them on the other side. Remarkably, some stay behind for a little female companionship. That's right, female companionship. One well-known romantic ghost can be found in Market Square Tavern on Duke of Gloucester Street.

After the battle, the wounded from both sides were taken into public buildings and private homes to have their wounds tended. Market Square Tavern was host to one young Confederate named Thomas Greeley. His wounds were too great, however, and he soon died. His body was taken from the tavern and buried in a mass grave outside town. Most people thought that was the last they would ever hear of Greeley. To the surprise of several pretty young women, this was not the case.

In 1952, Abigail Madison was a lovely young woman of nineteen. Arrangements had been made for her to spend the night at Market Square Tavern while visiting Williamsburg. Although nearly fifty years have passed, she vividly recalls her one night at the haunted lodging house.

"That day I traveled by train from Washington, D.C., to Colonial Williamsburg," Abigail explains. "I wasn't feeling well when I arrived, so I decided to take a nap in my hotel room before going sightseeing. I drew the drapes to make the room as dark as possible.

"I was almost asleep when I suddenly got the feeling that I wasn't alone. Even though the room was dark, I could see there was a man standing at the foot of my bed wearing a uniform—a Confederate uniform. I was too frightened to move, so I pretended that I was asleep. He didn't buy the act, though. He just stood there staring at me with a smile on his face.

"Then he began to move slowly around the side of my bed," Abigail continues. "He was coming closer with every step. When he was directly beside me, he reached out his hand as if he wanted to help me out of bed. It was then that I could see the light from a small crack in the curtains literally shine through him! Then he gave a slight bow and slowly faded away. I didn't believe in ghosts before then, but I certainly do now."

Since that time, there have been other accounts of the bold Thomas Greeley gazing upon fair young women in Market Square Tavern. Perhaps he's hoping that one day a pretty girl will take his hand and walk with him into the afterlife. Maybe then he wouldn't have to spend eternity alone.

Ghosts inhabit the College of William and Mary campus, where many wounded received treatment after the Battle of Williamsburg. Their reason for haunting the college is unknown. Could they be caught in a perpetual state of pain, or are they recovered and seeking to return to their cause?

The Long Lost Child
of the Powder Magazine

In Colonial Williamsburg, one gets the feeling of going back to the eighteenth century. Costumed interpreters walk the streets arguing the advantages of revolution. Horses pull oversize coaches, and children play with hoops from hogshead barrels. While strolling the ancient streets, it's easy to imagine bumping into Thomas Jefferson, Patrick Henry, or George Washington. These men spent a great deal of time in Williamsburg, as did anyone of importance during the colonial era.

Some of the finest examples of eighteenth-century architecture stand in Williamsburg: The College of William and Mary, the Governor's Palace, and the Capitol Building, among others. The past seems to come alive in Williamsburg—literally.

The Powder Magazine on Market Square is a prime example of these ghostly remnants. The octagonal brick building was erected in 1715 and has played an important roll in our country's history. At the onset of the Revolution, British troops raided the Powder Magazine and confiscated the town's muskets and ammunition. This act sent the citizens of Williamsburg into an uncontrollable rage.

A mob of one hundred fifty men, under the leadership of Patrick Henry, stormed the Governor's Palace and demanded the return of their arms. In fear for his life, the last Royal Governor of Virginia, Lord Dunmore, fled the back gates of the palace to board a boat on the James River. He headed for the safety of England, never to return to Virginia's shores.

Since its historic beginning, the Powder Magazine has served several purposes: a museum, a church for slaves, even a horse stable.

The octagonal brick wall surrounding the Powder Magazine was torn down in the mid-nineteenth century so the bricks could be used to build a church. This place of worship, the Greek Revival Baptist Church, stood next to the Magazine on Market Square. It was a big, beautiful building that also played a roll in history. Unfortunately, its contribution to the ages was a sad and bloody one.

After the Battle of Williamsburg, the church was used as a makeshift hospital for severely wounded Confederate soldiers. The blood was said to have run so heavily that it flowed down the marble steps onto the street. The church was later torn down, and the bricks were used to rebuild the wall surrounding the Magazine. While rebuilding the wall in the 1930s, a mass grave of two hundred Confederates was found near the Magazine's foundations.

With all the turbulence associated with the Powder Magazine and the wall surrounding it, one might think its ghost would be bold and brash. Perhaps he is the spirit of an aggressive British raider or the battered soul of a brutalized Confederate soldier. Surprisingly, this is not the case.

The ghost of a shy young girl in a pale blue dress has been seen hovering inside the Magazine. She holds a candle in her hand as she floats throughout the building. Her clothing is of the nineteenth century, and her hair is black and braided. She most often shows herself to other children. Unfortunately, this timid little ghost seems to be trapped in time, not knowing where her family has gone. Her plight is a sad one indeed.

Who this lonely child spirit is and why she lingers inside the Powder Magazine is a mystery. We can only hope that someday someone will return for her and place her into the loving arms of her long lost mother.

Massacre
at Martin's Hundreds

Almost four centuries ago, Captain John Smith wrote of the Virginia's Native Americans, "They drank a liquor of their own manufacture until they became sick. They seldom made war for land or goods, but principally for revenge. They are soon mounted to anger, and so malicious they seldom forgot an injury."

Needless to say, the first settlers on Virginia's shores lived in constant fear of losing their lives to the native inhabitants. In spite of repeated warnings, the people of Martin's Hundreds, a small settlement on the banks of the James River near Williamsburg, believed the local Indians to be their friends. The Powhatans were guests in their homes, ate their food, and slept in their beds. They exchanged knowledge and gifts on a regular basis.

The settlement of Martin's Hundreds lay hidden beneath the soil of Carters Grove Plantation for more than three centuries. It was lost in time until noted archeologist Ivor Noel Hume made an exciting but grisly discovery. While searching for a location suitable for the reception building of Carters Grove, he stumbled onto the remains of the 1619 settlement. On this site, two hundred twenty souls, having braved the long ocean voyage from England, settled their small township. The find was a great one indeed.

Hume also found disturbing evidence that Martin's Hundreds had all but perished in the Indian massacre of 1622. On the cold, foggy morning of March 22, the Powhatans made one great bloody attempt to rid the region of the settlers. In retaliation for the death of a warrior priest, they murdered every man, woman, and child they could find along the James and York Rivers. Although the citizens of Martin's Hundreds were innocent of the killing of the native priest, they were targeted for death.

Some of those participating in the killings had spent the night as guests in the homes of their intended victims. The settlers never suspected that their three-year friendship with the Indians had suddenly turned to hatred.

As Good Friday 1622 dawned, the Powhatans embarked upon their murderous spree. They killed one-fourth of the white population in the region and in the tiny township of Martin's Hundreds. The natives slaughtered the unsuspecting colonists with their own tools and utensils. The attack was well planned and merciless.

Several terrified citizens hid in the nearby woods, incapable of helping those left behind. They quietly watched as cries of agony rang out all around them. Some of the killers performed their gruesome tasks with calculated swiftness, while others used torture to prolong the suffering.

The Powhatans did not linger at the burned-out settlement, but rather moved on to other unsuspecting townships. They returned to Martin's Hundreds several hours later to loot the homes and mutilate their prey.

Those who survived the attack found their way back to the charred ruins of their small community, where they found their families, friends, and neighbors butchered. Disbelief filled their hearts. Scalps and other body parts had been taken. The Powhatans had also captured an estimated twenty prisoners from the settlement, fifteen of which were women.

Fearful of another attack, the settlers hastily buried their dead. Some simply threw dirt over the victims, not even taking the time to dig a grave.

Evidence suggests that some villagers gave their lives heroically. Lieutenant Richard Kean is said to have bravely remained behind to hold the gate of the fort closed, while others safely escaped out the back. He was then overtaken by several warriors and suffered multiple wounds. His body was discovered only a few feet from where the fort's gate once stood.

Another sad discovery was the body of a woman in her late thirties. After being held down and scalped, she ran panic-stricken from her home into a nearby ravine. She did not survive, likely due to blood loss. Her bones were found in a fetal position, with the bones of a tiny puppy at her feet.

Even now, an ominous feeling hovers in the air over the long-forgotten settlement. Hume has stated, "The past seems to linger in Martin's Hundreds." It's as if a thin veil shields us from witnessing the atrocities that transpired all those years ago on the banks of the James River.

While collecting information for the novel *Massacre at Martin's Hundreds*, I was unable to identify the scalped woman in the ravine. Frustrated, I approached the deserted gravesite, muttering to myself, "What was your name? What was your name?" It was then that I heard someone call out, "My name is Margaret," in a strong and offended manner. Her strange accent was not at all familiar.

Chills swept through my body. There was not a living soul in sight! I searched the entire area thoroughly and saw no one. The only explanation I can offer is that the voice was that of the woman in the ravine. Could her ghost have wandered the site of her death all these years?

Months later, while on one of my many visits to Martin's Hundreds, I had another odd experience. It was an overcast day in November, and I was strolling the peaceful grounds of Carters Grove. I was completely alone, the weather likely keeping others away that day.

As I followed the footpath near the river, rain began to fall. All at once, I heard the sounds of hammering and muffled voices. "Who could possibly be working outside in this weather?" I asked myself. A clump of trees blocked my view, so I couldn't tell what was happening. Perhaps laborers were working on the foundations of the old fort. I was excited by this notion, because I have always believed that more effort should be made to reveal the whole story of Martin's Hundreds.

The pounding sounds and voices grew louder the closer I got to the clearing. As I rounded the corner, I was shocked to find the grounds of the old fort quiet and empty. At that moment, I realized

Hume's statement was correct. Although I'm certain he didn't mean it literally, I (and probably others as well) feel the past really does linger in Martin's Hundreds.

A Mischievous Spirit
in Hampton

There are as many different types of ghosts as there are living people. Each ghost has its own separate and distinct personality. If a person was kind and loving in life, he or she is likely have that same disposition as a ghost.

The same can be said for someone who had a mischievous nature. As an apparition, he may be known to keep the same annoying traits. I came upon such a ghost a few years ago while managing a retirement home in Hampton, Virginia.

I had the use of a second-floor apartment above the elderly residents. During my stay there, I had the fortune to meet several interesting people who enthusiastically recounted stories of the past.

One such story concerned a former tenant who shot himself in the head in the parking lot. Before he was stricken with brain cancer, he was known to be a fun-loving soul. But as time passed, he could no longer bear the intense pain of his illness. One night the man sneaked out of the building and to the trunk of his car, where he had hidden a gun. When workers realized he was missing, they rushed outside only to see the most horrible sight they had ever witnessed. The elderly resident shot himself in the head and died instantly. Everyone stood silent, shocked and sickened.

Since that tragic night, those working and living at the home insist the spirit of the dead man has remained at the place where he spent his last days. Although I heard tell of the ghost on several occasions, I was not convinced that a spirit inhabited the building. It was only when strange things began happening inside my own apartment that I accepted the fact that the ghost truly did exist.

One morning, while I was in my first-floor office, my mother, Marlene, was upstairs diligently working on her book. She heard the door of the apartment open and then slam shut. The sound was unmistakable, because the door was made of heavy metal. It locked automatically, making it necessary to use a key to get inside. My mother and I were the only two people to have keys.

She called out several times, thinking it was I who had slammed the door. When I didn't answer, she got up to check the apartment but found no one. Nevertheless, the door was wide open. This happened throughout the day, alarming my mother greatly. As time went on, other mysterious events began to happen.

During my lunch break one afternoon, I retreated to the comfort of my apartment for some much-needed peace and quiet. I popped a frozen pizza into the oven and then watched television until my food was ready. I looked forward to the taste of fresh, hot pizza. Later, I found the oven had magically shut itself off. This happened time and time again in the following weeks. Equally strange, I often entered the apartment and found my refrigerator door wide open. After closing it, I would return to find it open once again.

The bathroom was also the scene of mischievous acts. During my showers, the bathtub drain usually closed off. The tub nearly overflowed by the time I finished my shower. The moment I stepped out of the tub, the water flowed freely down the drain again.

Soon after the bathtub incidents began, so did the unexplainable sound of a man's voice in the kitchen. My mother and I were awakened often by the voice, only to find no one in the apartment. There were nights that the voice was so loud, we could hardly get any rest at all.

Months after the peculiar events began, I left my job at the haunted retirement home. I could no longer live in an apartment that housed a mischievous spirit. Although the supernatural pranks must have seemed humorous to the retirement home's ghost, I didn't find them at all amusing.

Love Transcends Time at Biltmore House

Biltmore House, set among the rolling hills of Asheville, North Carolina, is the largest private residence in the United States. It was built for George Washington Vanderbilt, whose grandfather made the family fortune promoting railroads. After six years of construction, the grand mansion was completed in 1895. With two hundred fifty rooms, it was originally set on one hundred twenty-five thousand acres.

The elaborate home contained all the modern conveniences of the day—elevators, refrigeration, plumbing, and even electric lights. The front hall ceiling was an astonishing seventy-five feet high. Marble furnishings were placed throughout, and a spiral staircase surrounded a wrought iron chandelier. Leather lined the walls, magnificent art hung throughout the mansion, and the massive library contained twenty thousand volumes.

During the flamboyant Vanderbilt era, the estate was home to dozens of servants. Their comfortable accommodations were far above average for the times. Legend has it that the ghost of one of these servants is to this day living in the house.

In the early 1900s, a beautiful, golden-haired housemaid named Sarah lived at the estate. She fell deeply in love with Jonathan, a muscle-bound groundskeeper who also resided on the property.

The couple vowed to spend every free moment together. They rendezvoused in the gardens, out of everyone's sight. Because fraternization between coworkers was frowned upon, the young servants were forced to keep their love a secret.

The couple's undying affection for one another grew stronger as the years passed. They discussed marriage on several occasions but decided it would be a mistake. Neither owned a home, and their financial resources were virtually nonexistent. They felt that life at the estate was good, except for the fact that they could not share their love openly. The couple sincerely believed that someday they would leave Biltmore together.

While at work one evening, Sarah confided her secret to another employee. She had worked alongside this woman for almost a year and believed her to be a loyal friend. This misguided trust caused Sarah's world to begin crumbling. The woman betrayed her by telling her supervisor of the affair. When confronted, Sarah refused to reveal the name of her young lover. This was the end of poor Sarah's happiness. She was fired immediately and ordered off the property. Unbeknownst to Jonathan, Sarah left Biltmore in the dead of night.

The next morning, Jonathan learned of Sarah's hasty departure. He was devastated. He remained at the estate for several months, hoping Sarah would return. As time passed, he realized this was not to be. He gave up the security of Biltmore to search for his beloved Sarah. He roamed the countryside in a futile attempt to find his one true love.

Jonathan died two years later. The cause of death was listed as unknown. Not surprisingly, some believed he died of a broken heart. Nevertheless, no one could have foretold that Jonathan's ghost would return to Biltmore in an ongoing and desperate search for his fair-haired beauty.

Although almost a century has passed since this sad saga took place, people still report witnessing Jonathan's sorrowful spirit roaming the lush grounds of the estate. Sandy Crow claims to have encountered him in 1998.

"My mom and I came to Biltmore last spring," Sandy explains. "The place is amazing. Mom fell in love with the house, but I was more interested in the wonderful gardens. After a while, I left mom inside the mansion so I could take another walk around the property.

"The gardens were just so beautiful that I lost track of time," Sandy continues. "I wanted to see every single flower. I had been walking quite a while when I noticed a very handsome man following me. At first I was flattered, but the more he followed me the more scared I became.

"I headed for the house, and there he was, right behind me. When I began to walk faster, so did he. I think he thought I was somebody else, because he shouted the name 'Sarah.'

"I decided to take control of the situation, so I turned and faced him. I said, 'I'm not Sarah.' He bowed his head and said he was sorry. As he turned to walk away, he disappeared. I don't know how else to explain it. He just turned into a puff of smoke and vanished."

Other golden-haired beauties have run across the devoted spirit of the nineteenth-century Adonis. Most say they would be happy to take Sarah's place in Jonathan's heart. After all, who could resist playing a role in a fairy tale?

A Reunion with the Dead in Hendersonville

When I was seven, my parents divorced. Since I was an only child, I had no sibling to talk with about my confusion. There was no one to share my pain. I felt lost and desperately alone.

It was at my lowest point that I found a guardian angel, a woman in her late sixties who suffered from crippling arthritis. She was my maternal grandmother, Hazel. I loved her more than anyone could possibly imagine. She became my saving grace.

I was fortunate to spend a great deal of time with Hazel. To my delight, she entertained me for hours with tales of her wild teenage years. She was funny, warm, loving, and especially comforting.

While spending the night at Hazel's house, I often woke her with my crying. Despite her great pain from the arthritis, she climbed the staircase to see if I was all right. Her arthritis was so advanced that she slept on the couch instead of taking the stairs to her bedroom. By the time Hazel reached my bedroom, she was exhausted and wracked with pain.

I could hear her footsteps scraping against the floor as she came closer. Then I heard the doorknob slowly turn and saw the door open slightly. Hazel's little gray-haired head appeared in the doorway just above the knob. She always asked, "Honey, are you alright?" after which I replied, "Yes, Grandma, I'm fine." She then asked, "Are you sure?" Hazel never left until she was satisfied with my answer.

When I was fifteen years old, my mother and I moved from Glens Falls, New York, to Hendersonville, North Carolina. I only saw Hazel a couple of times after that. I missed her terribly. Two years later, Hazel died of heart failure. I was consumed with grief.

Several weeks after her death, I continued to cry myself to sleep each night.

Then one night, as I wept on my pillow, I heard the doorknob slowly turn. I was terrified because I thought I was alone in the house. The door opened slightly, and the light from the living room streamed into my darkened bedroom. I was too frightened to scream. I just lay there waiting for whomever the person was to enter. Little did I know I was in for the biggest surprise of my young life.

A little gray-haired head appeared in the doorway, and I heard a sweet voice say, "Honey, are you alright?" I replied, "Yes, Grandma, I'm fine." She asked, "Are you sure?" After I reassured her once again, she slowly backed away and closed the door.

Although stunned, I was filled with a sense of peace. I sincerely believed my loving grandmother would always be nearby. More than twenty years have passed since I saw the spirit of Hazel, but I remain convinced that if I ever need her, she will somehow be here for me.

After my parents divorced, my mother and I moved into an apartment. But I was unable to adjust to my new life. I did poorly in school, and missed my friends and father. My doctor said I needed to return to familiar surroundings. Reluctantly, my mother sent me back to live in my old house with my father, Jack, his new wife, and her daughter.

As time went on, tensions between my stepmother and me escalated into full-scale warfare. Four long years later, I left my father's unhappy home to once again live with my mother. My life took a dramatic turn for the better. As a result, I chose to spend little time with Jack. After my mother and I moved to Hendersonville, I saw him only a couple of times. Things between us seemed cold and distant. Then, shortly before his death, he pleaded with me for one more visit.

To my surprise, Jack was open, honest, giving, and even loving. It seemed he was trying to make amends for the past. We spent a week talking and getting to know one another. It was as if I finally had a father. Four months later, Jack died from a heart attack at the age of forty-four. I was terribly upset by his passing. We had just found each other, only to be separated again.

One sleepless night, shortly after Jack's death, I was again filled with grief. I wept openly, knowing no one was nearby to hear me. The light was on, and I wasn't at all drowsy. Suddenly, I heard the sliding glass door open. I was certain that I had locked it before going to bed. I thought, this couldn't be happening.

Then I saw a hand reach in and pull back the curtains. To my disbelief, Jack stepped inside. I lay there wide-eyed and speechless. He took two steps towards me and gave me a delightful smile. Jack looked wonderful! He looked at least fifteen years younger than when I had last seen him, just as he did while in his prime. He said, "Don't worry about me, kid. I'm happier than I've ever been." As he turned to leave, he glanced at me over his shoulder, and laughingly said, "Keep it light, kid." A moment later, he was gone.

I ran after him, but could see no sign that Jack had ever been there. I searched the grounds hoping for just one more glimpse of him. But I knew in my heart that Jack was gone for good.

I believe my father appeared to me that night to say in his own glib fashion that everything would be all right. Just as I remain certain that my dear grandmother Hazel will always be with me, I know that someday I will see Jack again, if not in this life, then another. It's only a matter of time.

Blackbeard's Ghost Wanders Ocracoke Island

The small island of Ocracoke, North Carolina, is eighteen miles long and one-half to two miles wide. The Atlantic Ocean and Pamlico Sound surround the tiny island. The turbulent seas off its eastern shore are commonly known as "the graveyard of the Atlantic." This rocky area earned its ominous title because of an abundance of shipwrecks spanning several centuries. Literally hundreds of sailing vessels have met their watery doom off the coast of Ocracoke Island.

The village of Ocracoke is located near the island's southern tip. Settled during the seventeenth century, it became a safe haven for pirates. All were known to rob and murder, but no pirate was more feared than Edward Teach, alias Blackbeard. It was on Ocracoke that Blackbeard spent his last days.

Teach is thought to have been born in Bristol, England, on or about the year 1680. It's rumored that he came from an influential family. Teach was an educated, intelligent man who read and wrote quite well—uncommon skills for pirates.

During Queen Anne's War, Teach served with boldness and courage aboard the ships of privateers. At that time, piracy was encouraged against the Spanish and sanctioned by the British government. It was plain to see that Teach very much enjoyed the excitement this type of lifestyle offered. Shortly after he left the navy, he struck up a friendship with the most feared pirate of the times, Benjamin Hornigold.

It was not long before Hornigold realized Teach had extraordinary abilities as a pirate. He was fearless, a cutthroat, and thrived on danger. Teach's large frame and aggressive nature set him apart from the others aboard ship.

After a particularly successful raid, Hornigold rewarded Teach by giving him a large ship they had seized. Soon after, the pair split company and Teach went out on his own.

He grew a waist length beard, which covered most of his face, and became commonly known as Blackbeard. He tied up his bushy whiskers in pigtails and fuse cords, lighting them as he approached passing vessels. He so frightened those aboard the opposing ships that they surrendered without a fight. The flamboyant pirate often forced the men of captured vessels to join his crew.

Blackbeard was known to shock all those around him by drinking a hardy brew of rum and gunpowder, which he lit before swallowing. He was also known to astound his men with deadly games. While he and his crew were below deck, Blackbeard closed the hatches and lit pots of combustible materials. His men nearly suffocated as a result of this prank. They ran for open air, leaving the unshakable Blackbeard behind.

Blackbeard invented another dangerous game, in which members of his crew were hung from a rope by the neck until almost dead. This game was intended to test his crewmen's courage and endurance. The pirate must have truly wanted his men to believe that he was the devil incarnate.

The infamous Blackbeard enjoyed living his life hard and fast. Although his career as a pirate lasted only a few short years, his fearsome reputation spread throughout the world. From his stronghold in the Bahamas, to America's eastern shores, Blackbeard terrified those traveling the high seas.

The troublesome pirate amassed such wealth from his raids that he stopped to bury his loot regularly. Ocracoke Island was said to have been his favorite place to hide gold, silver, and other valuables.

Blackbeard gave up pirating for a short period of time, however, and struck up an unlikely friendship with the governor of North Carolina, Charles Eden. Eden pardoned Blackbeard for his crimes and introduced him to the influential people living in the small borough of Bath Town. Blackbeard settled in Bath and married his fourteenth wife. He soon went back to his old ways, as life as a respectable citizen had grown tiresome for him and his men. They returned to the sea, tormenting those sailing off the shores of Virginia and North Carolina.

Many thought that Governor Eden and Chief Justice Tobias Knight profited from Blackbeard's pirating. Blackbeard was thought to have shared his stolen loot with Eden and Knight in return for free rein over North Carolina's waterways.

The people of North Carolina realized they could not count on their government to protect them from Blackbeard and his men. They soon grew so desperate that they turned to Governor Spottswood of the state of Virginia for help. To their relief, Spottswood took action.

In November 1718, Spottswood sent a floating search party of two sloops, led by Lieutenant Robert Maynard, after Blackbeard. Maynard found the notorious pirate at the southern tip of Ocracoke Island. Since Blackbeard had recently marooned a large portion of his crew on a deserted shore, he had as few as twenty-five men with which to do battle. Maynard's crew of more than fifty spent a long night preparing for the fight of their lives.

As the morning of November 22 dawned, Blackbeard and ten of his men boarded Maynard's ship, The Pearl. Thinking Maynard had a much smaller crew, Blackbeard was in for quite a surprise. A bloody fight ensued. The savage duel between Blackbeard and Maynard lasted more than two hours.

Blackbeard received twenty stab wounds and was shot five times, but still he continued fighting. It was only when Maynard's crew thought Blackbeard was close to death that they went to their leader's aid. The final blow came when Blackbeard's throat was cut from behind by one of Maynard's hesitant crewmen. The mighty Blackbeard fell dead.

Blackbeard's head was cut from his body and placed on the bowsprit of The Pearl. His body was then tossed overboard. While The Pearl remained offshore for the next two days, Blackbeard's decapitated body stayed afloat. It circled the ship continuously, horrifying both captives and victors alike. It was at this time that the rumor of Blackbeard's ghost began. From 1718 to the present, the frightening spirit of the bold pirate has haunted Ocracoke Island.

Throughout much of his life, Blackbeard sincerely believed that upon his death, the devil would be there to greet him. It was a meeting he was looking forward to with great anticipation. But without his head, how would the devil know who he was? For this reason, Blackbeard continues to search the island for his missing head.

The pirate's glowing apparition has been witnessed countless times, walking among the buildings in Ocracoke Village. His angry voice has been heard demanding the immediate return of his head. Although Blackbeard commanded much respect in life, his ghost sometimes receives little regard. It has become almost commonplace for villagers to see the headless spirit of the murderous pirate roaming their small town.

Sandy Vaughn is a longtime resident of Ocracoke. She claims to have witnessed Blackbeard's ghost walking along the deserted shoreline in the spring of 1998. "I always go for a walk along the beach before breakfast," Sandy explains. "This particular morning, I had to be to work early, so I took my walk before dawn. I'd walked a long way, so I decided to sit and rest while watching the sunrise.

"It was still dark when I noticed a glowing figure coming toward me. It was too far away for me to get a good look. As it got closer, I could tell that it was a large man—just the body—no head! One of my friends had told me he had seen the same thing once before, so I knew what to expect. He said it was the ghost of Blackbeard the pirate.

"I guess I should've run away, but I was too curious to leave. He passed right in front of me and acted like I wasn't even there. It was the weirdest thing. I knew if I waited long enough, someday I was bound to see him."

Others are not so nonchalant when they encounter the spectacle of Blackbeard's illuminated ghost. Pam Taylor, a one-time visitor to Ocracoke, tells of her frightening encounter with the dead pirate.

"I was having a great time until my third night on the island," Pam says. "I was asleep in my hotel room on the beach when a strange noise woke me up. It sounded like an animal howling.

"I looked out the window and saw a man standing with his back to me. I studied him for a minute because I couldn't figure out why he was all lit up. I thought he was looking down because I couldn't see his head. He stretched out his arms and let out an awful cry. Then I knew he wasn't looking down. He actually had no head! I was so surprised that I screamed really loud. When I screamed, he turned and faced me. He started walking toward me. I didn't know what to do so I hid in the closet. I was so scared. I was terrified that he would find me at any moment. I crouched down and waited, but he never came. I stayed in the closet until morning.

"Later, I told the guy at the front desk what happened. He said it was just the ghost of Blackbeard looking for his head. I checked out of my room and left the island and I've never been back since."

Charleston's Spirits Remain Where Their Bodies Lie

In April 1670, a tiny band of settlers landed on the banks of what later became South Carolina and formed a community called Charles Town, named after King Charles II. By 1680, the settlement proved too small for the influx of new residents, so the township moved onto a larger plot of land between the Cooper and Ashley Rivers.

Charles Town grew wealthy, thanks to its large cotton and rice plantations and an ideal location as a major seaport. But it was not without its troubles. The growing township was soon devastated by an outbreak of smallpox. Then fire destroyed a major portion of the city. Yellow Fever took its toll on the human population, and disease killed most of the cattle in the area. In addition, hurricanes plagued the region, claiming many lives.

Then in 1706 a fleet of French and Spanish seamen invaded Charles Town and demanded its surrender. The heroic Colonel William Rhett refused to acknowledge the commands of these invaders. Instead, Rhett armed a fleet of merchant ships and drove them from Charles Town's shores.

But Charles Town continued to be plagued by enemy forces from the sea. Pirates threatened all those sailing the Atlantic. They murdered, robbed, and pillaged their way along the East Coast. Charles Town proved a desirable target, with its prosperity and abundance of merchant vessels.

The most feared pirate of all time, Edward Teach, alias Blackbeard, was among those who terrorized the people of Charles

Town. He blockaded the Charles Town port with his fleet of six ships and captured numerous influential citizens. He threatened to kill the hostages and destroy the town if a chest of drugs was not delivered to him within two days. Charles Town later had its revenge with the hanging of an unprecedented forty-nine pirates, many of whom had sailed with Blackbeard.

War came to Charles Town in 1776. During the Revolution, more than two hundred British cannons fired upon Fort Moultrie, which guarded the seaport. After a nine-hour standoff, the English abandoned the attack. They made a second attempt to capture Charles Town in 1778 but were unsuccessful once again. In 1780 Charles Town finally succumbed to British advances. The enemy occupied the city for a year until the war ended in 1781.

After the British evacuation, the renamed city of Charleston evaded violent conflict for eight decades. Then the rumbles of war were felt once more. In April, 1861, the first shots of the Civil War were fired at Charleston's Fort Sumter. From that time forward, it was a downhill spiral for the war-torn city. Union forces bombarded the town with a steady stream of cannon fire. They burned and ravaged the region's magnificent homes.

Out of the ashes grew the beautiful Charleston of modern day. The scars of war and time are barely visible. Its citizens have managed to rebuild their city into one of the largest port towns on the Atlantic coast. The historic district is a marvel, and the economy is flourishing. Tourists flock to Charleston by the millions to relive its magnificent history. All is well in Charleston—or is it?

Major Stede Bonnet was a prosperous planter from Barbados. In 1717 he abandoned his wife and home for the thrill of adventure on the high seas. He later proved himself to be an inept pirate and an unwilling passenger on Blackbeard's ship. He was often seen walking about deck in his nightshirt.

Bonnet was among those hanged for piracy in Charleston. He begged for his life on the gallows but was refused clemency. He, along with the other forty-eight who hanged, was buried at White Point, now the site of the White Point Gardens in south Charleston.

Most people believe, however, that Bonnet's pitiful ghost wanders the site of his untimely death, still protesting his sad fate. His pleading figure has been witnessed time and time again at White Point Gardens.

Laura Paxton claims to have seen the portly ghost one day during the summer of 1997. "It was such a beautiful morning that my sister and I decided to tour White Point Park. We were looking out over the harbor when I felt someone tap me on the shoulder. When I turned around, I saw a man in a long white nightgown. I was shocked! My sister and I stood there speechless. I noticed his hands were folded in front of him like he was begging for something. A few seconds later he whispered, 'Help me, please.'

"When he saw that we couldn't do anything to help him, he walked past us toward the harbor. He walked to the edge and kept right on going! Then he was gone. We looked out over the water, but there was no trace of him. I felt so sorry for him that I cried.

"We ran to tell somebody what had happened. When we found someone who worked there, she told us this sort of thing has happened before. She said it was only a ghost. At that point, I didn't know who was crazier, the woman, for believing in ghosts, or us, for seeing him in the first place."

It's sad to think poor Stede Bonnet continues to pay the penalty for his brief time as a pirate. It is as if he's destined to spend his days begging for a second chance to be a good citizen. His spirit doesn't seem to realize the punishment for his crimes took place centuries ago.

Fort Moultrie plays host to another Charleston ghost. This spirit is not from the time of the American Revolution. Although the fort was involved in the bloody struggle for freedom, it has served other purposes. It was used as a place of incarceration for the chief of the Florida Seminole Indians, Osceola. Osceola spent his last days at Fort Moultrie. His grave is near the main portal.

Throughout the years, tourists and townspeople alike have witnessed the ghostly figure of the Seminole chief. His angry spirit seems bent on revenge for his imprisonment. The difference between this ghost and many others is the way he presents himself. You cannot see him with the naked eye, but he will show up in the lens of a camera.

John Oakdale of Atlanta visited Fort Moultrie last autumn. "I was taking pictures inside the fort," John says. "Everything seemed normal until I tried to take a picture inside the room where the Indian chief stayed. I looked through the viewfinder of my camera and saw him [Osceola] standing right in front of me! I couldn't believe it!

"I tried to take a picture, but my camera wouldn't work. When I lowered the camera, the Indian was gone. When I looked through the viewfinder again, there he was. I tried to take the picture over and over again, but my camera just wouldn't work. I began to think, what the heck am I still doing here. My better judgment told me to run, but instead I decided to take one more look. I put the camera to my eye and got the surprise of my life. There was the Indian chief standing three feet away! Suddenly, he leapt at me. I have to admit I was scared to death. I screamed and ran away.

"I was so embarrassed. Everybody was looking at me. I can't imagine what they all thought of me. I must've looked like a raving lunatic. I tried to compose myself and quietly leave the fort, which I did. When I got outside, I tried to use my camera again. This time, it was working just fine."

The ghosts of Charleston seem to haunt the grounds where their bodies lie. Visitors should consider a visit to the city's historic graveyards. Who knows what haunting figures they might hold.

Hauntings in Atlanta's Cemeteries

Atlanta has undergone many changes on its way to becoming a thriving metropolis. In the 1700s, the Cherokees occupied it. That changed when the area became a frontier outpost shortly after the arrival of the white man. By 1840, a railroad had been built, bringing with it a new population. This growth was far from peaceful.

Mounting tensions with the Cherokees made the white men determined to drive them from their homeland. The state ordered that most Cherokee farmland be given to Georgian settlers. Thousands of Cherokees were forced at gunpoint to move eight hundred miles westward to Oklahoma. A total of more than four thousand Cherokees died on the journey called the Trail of Tears. It was indeed a shameful time in our nation's history.

Shortly afterward, Atlanta, then called Terminus, became a meeting point for America's major railroads. From the rural hamlet, a bustling city quickly emerged. Terminus was renamed Marthasville, which became Atlanta in 1845.

After Georgia seceded from the Union to join forces with the Confederacy, Atlanta became a major Confederate military post because of its abundance of railroads linking the southern states. It wasn't long before the city seemed to grow into one large hospital. Trains carried hundreds of sick and wounded Confederates into town almost daily.

The Union realized it had to destroy Atlanta to win the war. In 1864, Major General William T. Sherman, under orders to inflict as much damage on Atlanta as possible, marched toward the city. Sherman's forces, numbering more than a hundred thousand, moved against sixty thousand Confederates. During the course of several bloody battles, the Rebels lost three men to every one Federal soldier killed.

As the sweltering summer of 1864 got underway, Atlanta was continuously bombarded by Union artillery. The death toll was staggering. Federal forces destroyed area railroads, cutting off supplies to Atlanta citizens. If starvation and lack of medicine didn't kill them, the fires certainly would.

On August 9, 1864, Union artillery fire intensified, turning parts of Atlanta into raging infernos. There were so many fires that they lit up the night sky for miles.

Atlanta's citizens were in a desperate situation. They tried every means to escape. As panic mounted, numerous townspeople turned against one another. Looting and robbery grew out of control.

By September 2, the citizens could take no more. A white flag was raised, officially surrendering Atlanta to the Union. Federal troops quickly took control of the city. They forced people from their homes, leaving them sick and destitute.

Before departing in November, Federals torched the entire city. Virtually nothing remained standing. The once-great metropolis was reduced to a pile of ashes. Nevertheless, its people slowly returned to rebuild their shattered lives.

Today, the city's many ghosts are reminders of Atlanta's eventful past. Dozens of Civil War spirits are said to roam the streets, homes, public buildings, and especially cemeteries. Oakland Cemetery is thought to be one of the most active sites.

The eighty-eight acres of Oakland Cemetery serve as the final resting place for both Confederate and Union dead. Trees used to hang Federal raiders can be seen from the rolling lawn. From the limb of one of these trees, a man's lifeless body, dressed in blue, has been witnessed dangling. This morbid sight has shocked residents for over a century.

One elderly woman who wishes to remain anonymous has shared a letter written to her mother by her grandmother in 1891. It states, "My dearest daughter, I must confess to you a vision, so disturbing in nature, that I cannot dismiss it from my memory. While placing a wreath upon Uncle Andrew's grave, I witnessed a man hanging from a tree. This ghastly scene was such a shock to me, that it took several minutes to recuperate my normal functions.

"His dress was not of today, but of the style of the war. I believed him a Yank, and still I felt grieved. I averted my eyes as I thought the sight might make me ill. Upon looking back, the spectacle was gone. I can only tell you of this my dear daughter, as I fear everyone else would believe me insane."

Why the Union soldier's lifeless body remains at the place of his painful death is unknown. It is sad to see, after so many years, that he is literally suspended in time.

Another Civil War ghost of Oakland Cemetery is said to lie atop his own grave. This Confederate soldier looks as if he's peacefully sleeping, only to disappear when witnesses approach.

Young Blair Breckenridge claims to have seen this spirit, known as "the sleeping soldier." Blair describes, "I was at the cemetery to put flowers on my grandfather's grave. It looked like it was going to rain, so I wasn't planning to stay very long. I put the flowers down and said a prayer over my grandfather and then I turned to leave. After I walked a couple hundred yards, I saw a man lying on the ground. It looked like he was taking a nap. I didn't want to wake him, so I walked as quietly as I could.

"As I got closer to him, I could tell he was badly hurt," Blair continues. "I saw blood literally pouring out of his chest! I knew if he didn't get help soon, he would die. I ran over to him to see if I could do something. Suddenly his eyes popped open. He turned his head and looked at me. His eyes were like nothing I'd ever seen before. They were hollow. He had no eyes! Then he slowly turned his head away and disappeared. It was the most awful thing I'd ever seen. If that's what the cemetery is like during the daytime, I'd hate to be there at night."

The witnesses who have seen Atlanta's Civil War ghosts come in all ages. People who have lived a century apart relate similar haunting tales. Perhaps one hundred years from now, others will be telling the same supernatural stories of Atlanta's turbulent past.

Atlanta's cemeteries are home to numerous ghosts from throughout the city's history. Trees on the rolling acres of Oakland Cemetery were used to hang Federal raiders. Perhaps these ghosts, captured at night inside the cemetery, are all that remain of the unlucky soldiers.

Hauntings are Plentiful at Castillo de San Marcos

Beautiful St. Augustine, Florida, grew from conflict. In 1564, Fort Caroline was built to protect the small colony of French Protestants who had settled in the region. But Spanish raiders, led by Pedro Menendez de Aviles, laid waste to the town. They captured Fort Caroline and killed one hundred forty Frenchmen in the process. All French soldiers who were found in the area were beheaded.

In 1586, the English corsair, Sir Francis Drake, and two thousand of his men took control of St. Augustine. Its townspeople were terrified. Sadly, their worst nightmares came true. Without mercy, Drake burned Fort Caroline to the ground.

By 1672, the people of St. Augustine decided it was in their best interest to replace their wooden fort with a stone one. They called it, Castillo de San Marcos. Its walls were ten feet thick and as much as twenty-five feet high in some areas. This impervious structure took twenty-three years to build.

Throughout the colonial era, Castillo de San Marcos changed hands several times. In the 1830s it became a military post used to imprison rebellious Seminole Indians. By the 1860s, it was occupied by the Union Army.

Not surprisingly, human bones have been discovered in the foundations of the old fort. Authorities believe people who displeased its early leaders were sealed inside the walls, leaving them to die a lingering death. Given its cruel and turbulent past, Castillo de San Marcos is known to hold tormented souls of long ago.

From time to time, a glowing figure of a man appears in the dungeon area. It motions for people to follow him as he passes through the wall. Perhaps he's looking for a savior to release him from the lonely tomb. His physical bondage of stone seems to keep his spirit trapped, unaware that he can leave any time he chooses.

Samuel Clarke is but one of many to claim they have seen the illuminated spirit of Castillo de San Marcos. During his first visit to St. Augustine, in the spring of 1991, he and his girlfriend, Sarah, encountered the glowing apparition. "Sarah thought it would be romantic to walk the grounds of the old fort just before sunset," Samuel says. "As we were about to leave, Sarah said she heard a man whispering from around the corner. She pulled me by the hand to see who it was.

"As we rounded the corner of the fort, we saw a man motioning for us to follow him. He was so bright; I could swear he was on fire. Needless to say, we didn't move. It looked like he was getting angry because we wouldn't follow him. Finally he gave up. He turned and walked right through the wall and vanished. Sarah and I couldn't believe what we had just seen. After we got over the shock, we ran as fast as our legs could carry us."

Another frightening apparition has been known to surprise visitors at Castillo de San Marcos. A flamboyant Indian can sometimes be seen leaping from the fort's protective outer walls. It looks as if he deliberately falls onto unsuspecting passersby. Some say he's covered with red paint, while others believe he is dripping with blood. The native spirit gives a chilling shriek as he plummets toward the earth. Perhaps he died while attempting to escape the stone walls.

In the autumn of 1988, Patrick Sherbet and his daughter, Carrie, were almost struck by the mysterious Indian. "Carrie and I were walking around the fort early one evening," Patrick says. "Nothing much was going on. There weren't very many people around, so it was pretty quiet.

"Suddenly we heard a horrible scream," Patrick continues. "We couldn't really tell where it came from. Then we heard another scream coming from above us. We looked up and saw a half-naked man jump from the top of the wall. He was falling right down on top of us! We covered our heads and waited, but nothing happened. I looked up and he was gone.

"The next morning, I thought we'd imagined the whole thing until I told one of the people working at the fort what had happened. She laughed and said, 'Oh that was just our Indian ghost. Don't worry, he wont hurt you.' I was glad she said that, because I was beginning to think we were a little nuts."

The spirited Indian seems destined to relive his horrifying death over and over again. Perhaps he remains oblivious to the fact that his first attempt at escape met with deadly consequences.

While touring the seventeenth-century fort, I also experienced a strange phenomenon. In the summer of 1986, my boyfriend, John, and I were exploring Castillo de San Marcos' watchtower. We could see most all of St. Augustine from where we stood. It was a beautiful day, although it was a little warm for my taste. The tower suddenly filled with ice-cold air. It was ninety-eight degrees outside, but we were shivering inside the tower.

The feeling that we were intruding on someone's domain overwhelmed John and me. We had a powerful sensation that we should leave immediately. It was as if someone were shouting in our ears, "Get out of here!"

After we left Castillo de San Marcos, we glanced up at the ominous watchtower. We saw a man wearing a red-and-gold hat looking down on us. This was odd, because we were among the last people to leave the fort that afternoon. No one should have been left inside. We later realized we hadn't seen any tourists wearing such a hat all day. Believe me, we certainly would have noticed.

John surmised the unusual man was the ghost of a Spanish guard still looking for the enemy, continuing with his duties more than four hundred years after his death. Although John and I disagreed about many things, in this case I have to admit I felt he was right.

About the Author

Jackie Eileen Behrend, author, historian, and photographer, was born in Glens Falls, New York. As a young girl she moved with her mother to Hendersonville, North Carolina, where she graduated high school at East Henderson High. Although schooled in business in college, Jackie's interest in history grew when she moved to Williamsburg, Virginia. Her subsequent research led to her book *The Hauntings of Williamsburg, Yorktown, and Jamestown* (John Blair), a combination of history and folklore set in Virginia's historic triangle. For this work she was nominated by The Library of Virginia as author of the best nonfiction book in the state. Jackie later brought the ghost stories in the book to life via her popular candlelit walking tour of Colonial Williamsburg.

Jackie Behrend now lives in Ocean Pines, Maryland, where she conducts for visitors her latest ghost tour, The Ghosts of Ocean City and Berlin.